BIBLE WISDOM
for Parents

COMPILED BY GARY WILDE

Christian
Parenting
B O O K S

All Scripture quotations are from the *Holy Bible: New International Version* ©1973, 1978, 1984 by International Bible Society. Used by permission of Zondervan Bible Publishers.

Christian Parenting Books is an imprint of
Chariot Family Publishing,
a div. of David C. Cook Publishing Co.
David C. Cook Publishing Co., Elgin, Illinois 60120
David C. Cook Publishing Co., Weston, Ontario
Nova Distribution Ltd., Newton Abbot, England

Christian Parenting Today Magazine
P.O. Box 850, Sisters, OR 97759 (800) 238-2221

BIBLE WISDOM FOR PARENTS
©1993 by Chariot Family Publishing

Cover design by Foster Design Associates
Interior Design by Glass House Graphics
Compiled by Gary Wilde

First Printing, 1993
Printed in the United States of America
97 96 95 94 93 5 4 3 2 1

CIP Applied for.
ISBN 0-78140-071-6

═══ TABLE OF CONTENTS ═══

CHAPTER 1   **11**

'Will I be able to keep my family founded on spiritual priorities?'

Build Your Home on a Solid Foundation of Biblical Principles

Accepting God's Sovereignty in Your Family

Bequeath Spiritual Priorities to Your Kids
- Teach Your Kids to Love God's Word
- Teach Your Kids to Pray
- Lead Your Kids to Jesus

Help Your Kids Know Their Awesome God
- He Is All-Powerful
- He Is All-Knowing and Wise
- He Is Patient
- He Is Merciful
- He Is Faithful

Teach Your Kids About Jesus

CHAPTER 2   **29**

'What can I do about a home environment that falls far short of 'heaven on earth'?'

Your Home Environment Is Crucial to Kids' Self-esteem

- Do You Communicate Lovingly?
- Is God Loved In Your Home?
- Is God the Ultimate Provider for the Family?
- Do You Offer Christian Hospitality from Your Home?
- Do You Maintain High Standards of Sexual Fidelity?

Kids Need to Know Their Parents are Still in Love

- Husband, Do You Adore Your Wife?
- Wife, Do You Adore Your Husband?

CHAPTER 3   47
'How can I build my child's self-esteem?'
Bless Your Children, Face to Face:

Tell of God's Blessings, Too:

- Honored In Creation
- Given a Mission In the Kingdom
- Blameless In God's Sight
- Created for Blessing
- Heirs to a Crown

CHAPTER 4   65
'Why am I always yelling at the kids?'
Teach and Train Your Children

- Help Them Accept Your Correction
- Accept God's Correction In Your Life, Too
- Help Them Learn to Persevere

- Help Them Resist Their Temptations
- Help Them Develop Good Work Habits
- Help Them Develop Self-discipline and Trustworthiness
- Help Them Get Along with One Another

Use Punishment Wisely

CHAPTER 5   83

'What are the lasting values to give my children?'

Biblical Values to Teach Your Children
- Compassion
- Faith
- Wisdom
- Obedience to God
- Forgiveness
- Honesty
- Humility
- Peacefulness
- Thoughtfulness
- Happiness

Biblical Values Stand Out In Our Society

Prepare for Opposition to Your Family's Values

CHAPTER 6   99

'What do I do when I feel frustrated with my parenting responsibilities?'

Beware Parenting Burnout

Give God Your Fears

Deal with Your Frustrations Properly

Don't Let Worry Take Over

You Are Not a Failure
- Accept Your Limitations
- Seek God's Peace

CHAPTER 7   **115**

'Where will the money come from, Lord?'

When Your Family Expenses Weigh You Down . . .
- Trust in God's Provision
- Honor God with Your Money
- Don't Make Money Your Primary Concern
- Don't Covet What Others Have
- Try to Help Others in Need, Too

CHAPTER 8   **131**

'Why do I feel so alone in my parenting struggles?'

Feeling Lonely As a Parent?
- Build a Support Network of Other Parents
- Find Support in Your Church
- Support One Another with Your Gifts

Learn to Fellowship with God in Prayer
- God Hears Your Prayers
- God's Spirit Dwells Within You

CHAPTER 9   149
'What do I do when parenting stress builds up?'

Look at the Sources of Your Stress
- Work Overload
- Family Tensions
- Church Disputes
- Neighbors at Odds
- Project Frustrations

Take Care of Yourself!
- Through Guarding Your Schedule
- Through Getting Enough Rest
- Through Asking God for Help

CHAPTER 1

'Will I be able to keep my family founded on spiritual priorities?'

There's just so much taking up a family's time these days," said Bob. His wife Claire added, "Even when we determine to have family devotions or get involved in a church program, our plans can be thwarted at the last minute; something unexpected comes up at school or the kids have made other plans with their friends.

"That's why we've been trying to view spiritual priorities as part of our normal, everyday life, rather than thinking it's always something we plan in a formal way. Actually, we can see that our life with the Lord is a relationship we model in lots of ways within our

11

family. We figure the kids are learning about the Lord whenever they observe how two of His children—Claire and I—act and react in everyday situations."

FOR MEMORY:

May I never boast except in the cross of our Lord Jesus Christ, through which the world has been crucified to me, and I to the world.

Galatians 6:14

FOR SILENT REFLECTION:

- *When I think about my life goals and dreams, where does God fit in?*

- *What are my dreams for my family?*

- *Do my children value the Bible and prayer? Why, or why not?*

- *To what extent have my kids' devotional attitudes been formed by observing my own priorities?*

Build Your Home on a Solid Foundation of Biblical Principles

"Therefore everyone who hears these words of mine and puts them into practice is like a wise man who built his house on the rock. The rain came down, the streams rose, and the winds blew and beat against that house; yet it did not fall, because it had its foundation on the rock. But everyone who hears these words of mine and does not put them into practice is like a foolish man who built his house on sand. The rain came down, the streams rose, and the winds blew and beat against that house, and it fell with a great crash."

When Jesus had finished saying these things, the crowds were amazed at his teaching.

Matthew 7:24-28

For no one can lay any foundation other than the one already laid, which is Jesus Christ. If any man builds on this foundation using gold, silver, costly stones, wood, hay or straw, his work will be shown for what it is, because the Day will bring it to light. It will be revealed with fire, and the fire will test the quality of each man's work. If what he has built survives, he will receive his reward.

I Corinthians 3:11-14

13

You also, like living stones, are being built into a spiritual house to be a holy priesthood, offering spiritual sacrifices acceptable to God through Jesus Christ.

I Peter 2:5

Therefore let us leave the elementary teachings about Christ and go on to maturity, not laying again the foundation of repentance from acts that lead to death, and of faith in God.

Hebrews 6:1

Do not deceive yourselves. If any one of you thinks he is wise by the standards of this age, he should become a "fool" so that he may become wise. For the wisdom of this world is foolishness in God's sight. As it is written: "He catches the wise in their craftiness."

I Corinthians 3:18, 19

The kingdom of the world has become the kingdom of our Lord and of his Christ, and he will reign for ever and ever.

Revelation 11:15

Accepting God's Sovereignty in Your Family

O Sovereign LORD, you have begun to show to your servant your greatness and your strong hand. For what god is there in heaven or on earth who can do the deeds and mighty works you do?

Deuteronomy 3:24

The heavens are yours, and yours also the earth; you founded the world and all that is in it.

Psalm 89:11

By wisdom the LORD laid the earth's foundations,
by understanding he set the heavens in place;
By his knowledge the deeps were divided,
and the clouds let drop the dew.

Proverbs 3:19, 20

For a man's ways are in full view of the LORD,
and he examines all his paths.

Proverbs 5:21

Death and Destruction lie open before the LORD—
how much more the hearts of men!

Proverbs 15:11

Then I heard what sounded like a great multitude, like the roar of rushing waters and like loud peals of thunder, shouting: "Hallelujah! For our Lord God Almighty reigns.

Revelation 19:6

Bequeath Spiritual Priorities to Your Kids

• *Teach Your Kids to Love God's Word*

I have hidden your word in my heart
that I might not sin against you. . . .
I delight in your decrees;
I will not neglect your word. . . .
Then I will answer the one who taunts me,
for I trust in your word. . . .
My comfort in my suffering is this:
Your promise preserves my life.

Psalm 119:11-50

Your word is a lamp to my feet
and a light for my path. . . .
Sustain me according to your promise, and I will live;
do not let my hopes be dashed. . . .
Direct my footsteps according to your word;
let no sin rule over me. . . .
Your promises have been thoroughly tested,

and your servant loves them. . . .
I rise before dawn and cry for help;
I have put my hope in your word.
My eyes stay open through the watches of the night,
that I may meditate on your promises. . . .
Defend my cause and redeem me;
preserve my life according to your promise.

Psalm 119:105-154

For the word of God is living and active. Sharper than any double-edged sword, it penetrates even to dividing soul and spirit, joints and marrow; it judges the thoughts and attitudes of the heart. Nothing in all creation is hidden from God's sight Everything is uncovered and laid bare before the eyes of him to whom we must give account.

Hebrews 4:12, 13

Be diligent in these matters; give yourself wholly to them, so that everyone may see your progress.

I Timothy 4:15

•*Teach Your Kids to Pray*
This is the confidence we have in approaching God: that if we ask anything according to his will, he hears us.

I John 5:14

17

Before they call I will answer; while they are still speaking I will hear.

Isaiah 65:24

Through Jesus, therefore, let us continually offer to God a sacrifice of praise—the fruit of lips that confess his name.

Hebrews 13:15

The end of all things is near. Therefore be clear minded and self-controlled so that you can pray.

I Peter 4:7

And pray in the Spirit on all occasions with all kinds of prayers and requests. With this in mind, be alert and always keep on praying for all the saints.

Ephesians 6:18

Let us draw near to God with a sincere heart in full assurance of faith, having our hearts sprinkled to cleanse us from a guilty conscience and having our bodies washed with pure water.

Hebrews 10:22

Ask and it will be given to you; seek and you will find; knock and the door will be opened to you. For everyone who asks receives; he who seeks finds; and to him who knocks, the door will be opened. Which of you, if his son asks for bread, will give him a stone?

Or if he asks for a fish, will give him a snake? If you, then, though you are evil, know how to give good gifts to your children, how much more will your Father in heaven give good gifts to those who ask him!

Matthew 7:7-11

• Lead Your Kids to Jesus

At that time the disciples came to Jesus and asked, "Who is the greatest in the kingdom of heaven?" He called a little child and had him stand among them. And he said: "I tell you the truth, unless you change and become like little children, you will never enter the kingdom of heaven. Therefore, whoever humbles himself like this child is the greatest in the kingdom of heaven. And whoever welcomes a little child like this in my name welcomes me.

Matthew 18:1-5

Come to me, all you who are weary and burdened, and I will give you rest. Take my yoke upon you and learn from me, for I am gentle and humble in heart,

19

and you will find rest for your souls. For my yoke is easy and my burden is light.

Matthew 11:28-30

You see, at just the right time, when we were still powerless, Christ died for the ungodly. Very rarely will anyone die for a righteous man, though for a good man someone might possibly dare to die. But God demonstrates his own love for us in this: While we were still sinners, Christ died for us. Since we have now been justified by his blood, how much more shall we be saved from God's wrath through him! For if, when we were God's enemies, we were reconciled to him through the death of his Son, how much more, having been reconciled, shall we be saved through his life!

Romans 5:6-10

Helping Your Kids Know Their Awesome God

• *He Is All-Powerful*
The LORD is my strength and my shield;
my heart trusts in him, and I am helped.
My heart leaps for joy
and I will give thanks to him in song.
The LORD is the strength of his people,
a fortress of salvation for his anointed one.

Psalm 28:7, 8

The LORD is slow to anger and great in power;
the LORD will not leave the guilty unpunished.
His way is in the whirlwind and the storm,

and clouds are the dust of his feet.
He rebukes the sea and dries it up;
he makes all the rivers run dry.
Bashan and Carmel wither
and the blossoms of Lebanon fade.
The mountains quake before him
and the hills melt away.
The earth trembles at his presence,
the world and all who live in it.
Who can withstand his indignation?
Who can endure his fierce anger?
His wrath is poured out like fire;
the rocks are shattered before him.

Nahum 1:3-6

What, then, shall we say in response to this? If God
is for us, who can be against us?

Romans 8:31

• He Is All-Knowing and Wise
By his knowledge the deeps were divided,
and the clouds let drop the dew.

Proverbs 3:20

21

"For my thoughts are not your thoughts,
neither are your ways my ways," declares the LORD.

Isaiah 55:8

"Praise be to the name of God for ever and ever; wisdom and power are his. He changes times and seasons; he sets up kings and deposes them. He gives wisdom to the wise and knowledge to the discerning. He reveals deep and hidden things; he knows what lies in darkness, and light dwells with him.

Daniel 2:20-22

For the foolishness of God is wiser than man's wisdom, and the weakness of God is stronger than man's strength.

I Corinthians 1:25

And even the very hairs of your head are all numbered.

Matthew 10:30

• *He Is Patient*

Rend your heart and not your garments. Return to the LORD your God, for he is gracious and compassionate, slow to anger and abounding in love, and he relents from sending calamity.

Joel 2:13

Or do you show contempt for the riches of his kindness, tolerance and patience, not realizing that God's kindness leads you toward repentance?

Romans 2:4

• He Is Merciful

You are a forgiving God, gracious and compassionate, slow to anger and abounding in love. Therefore you did not desert them . . . and when they cried out to you again, you heard from heaven, and in your compassion you delivered them time after time.

You warned them to return to your law, but they became arrogant and disobeyed your commands. They sinned against your ordinances, by which a man will live if he obeys them. Stubbornly they turned their backs on you, became stiff-necked and refused to listen.

For many years you were patient with them. By your Spirit you admonished them through your prophets. Yet they paid no attention, so you handed them over to the neighboring peoples. But in your great mercy you did not put an end to them or abandon them, for you are a gracious and merciful God.

Numbers 9:17b-31

For this is what the high and lofty One says—
he who lives forever, whose name is holy:
"I live in a high and holy place,
but also with him who is contrite and lowly in spirit,

to revive the spirit of the lowly
and to revive the heart of the contrite.
I will not accuse forever,
nor will I always be angry,
for then the spirit of man would grow faint before
me—
the breath of man that I have created.
I was enraged by his sinful greed;
I punished him, and hid my face in anger,
yet he kept on in his willful ways.
I have seen his ways, but I will heal him;
I will guide him and restore comfort to him,
creating praise on the lips of the mourners in Israel.
Peace, peace, to those far and near,"
says the LORD. "And I will heal them."

Isaiah 57:15-19

Be merciful, just as your Father is merciful.

Luke 6:36

• He Is Faithful

Whenever the rainbow appears in the clouds, I will see it and remember the everlasting covenant between God and all living creatures of every kind on the earth.

Genesis 9:16

Lift up your eyes to the heavens,
look at the earth beneath;
the heavens will vanish like smoke,
the earth will wear out like a garment
and its inhabitants die like flies.
But my salvation will last forever,
my righteousness will never fail. . . .
For the moth will eat them up like a garment;
the worm will devour them like wool.
But my righteousness will last forever,
my salvation through all generations."

Isaiah 51:6-8

God is not unjust; he will not forget your work and the love you have shown him as you have helped his people and continue to help them. . . .

When God made his promise to Abraham, since there was no one greater for him to swear by, he swore by himself, saying, "I will surely bless you and give you many descendants." And so after waiting patiently, Abraham received what was promised. Men swear by someone greater than themselves, and the oath confirms what is said and puts an end to all argument. Because God wanted to make the unchanging nature of his purpose very clear to the heirs of what was promised, he confirmed it with an oath. God did this so that, by two unchangeable things in which it is impossible for God to lie, we who have fled to take hold of the hope offered to us may be greatly encouraged. We have this hope as an anchor for the soul, firm and secure. It enters the inner sanctuary behind the curtain.

Hebrews 6:10-19

So then, those who suffer according to God's will should commit themselves to their faithful Creator and continue to do good.

I Peter 4:19

Teach Your Kids About Jesus

In the beginning was the Word, and the Word was with God, and the Word was God. . . . The Word became flesh and made his dwelling among us. We have seen his glory, the glory of the One and Only, who came from the Father, full of grace and truth.

John 1:1-14

Who, being in very nature God, did not consider equality with God something to be grasped.

Philippians 2:6

Beyond all question, the mystery of godliness is great: He appeared in a body, was vindicated by the

Spirit, was seen by angels, was preached among the nations, was believed on in the world, was taken up in glory.

I Timothy 3:16

It is because of him that you are in Christ Jesus, who has become for us wisdom from God—that is, our righteousness, holiness and redemption.

I Corinthians 1:30

Therefore I will give him a portion among the great, and he will divide the spoils with the strong, because he poured out his life unto death, and was numbered with the transgressors. For he bore the sin of many,

27

and made intercession for the transgressors.

Isaiah 53:12

God made him who had no sin to be sin for us, so that in him we might become the righteousness of God.

II Corinthians 5:21

He himself bore our sins in his body on the tree, so that we might die to sins and live for righteousness; by his wounds you have been healed. For you were like sheep going astray, but now you have returned to the Shepherd and Overseer of your souls.

I Peter 2:24, 25

FOR PERSONAL PRAYER:

Lord, with everything around me that clamors for my attention, please give me the calmness to remember that You dwell inside of me. As I seek Your guidance throughout this day, help me to live by the principles You've set for me in Your Word, that I might model Your priorities for my children. Amen.

CHAPTER 2

'What can I do about a home environment that falls far short of 'heaven on earth'?

"They say the hardest place to be a Christian is in your own home, among your own family members," said Don "I guess I'd have to agree with that. I'd hate for anyone to see what it's really like sometimes in our home.

"I mean, around other people, you're usually putting your best foot forward. But with my kids and wife, I know my temper can flare, or my moods can get everybody else feeling down."

FOR MEMORY:

May the God who gives endurance and encouragement give you a spirit of unity among yourselves as you follow Christ Jesus, so that with one heart and mouth you may glorify the God and Father of our Lord Jesus Christ.

Romans 15:5, 6

FOR SILENT REFLECTION:

- *How much difference is there in my "public Christianity" and my private walk with the Lord?*

- *What effect is this difference having on my children?*

- *In what key areas could my family members improve in relating lovingly with each other?*

- *What is the first step for me, personally, to take in this regard?*

Your Home Environment Is Crucial to Kids' Self-esteem

• Do You Communicate Lovingly?

Speaking the truth in love, we will in all things grow up into him who is the Head, that is, Christ. From him the whole body, joined and held together by every supporting ligament, grows and builds itself up in love, as each part does its work.

Ephesians 4:15, 16

Speak to one another with psalms, hymns and spiritual songs. Sing and make music in your heart to the Lord, always giving thanks to God the Father for everything, in the name of our Lord Jesus Christ.

Ephesians 5:19, 20

Carry each other's burdens, and in this way you will fulfill the law of Christ. If anyone thinks he is something when he is nothing, he deceives himself. Each one should test his own actions. Then he can take pride in himself, without comparing himself to somebody else.

Galatians 6:2-4

Be completely humble and gentle; be patient, bearing with one another in love. Make every effort to keep the unity of the Spirit through the bond of peace.

-Ephesians 4:2, 3

• *Is God Loved in Your Home?*

Know therefore that the LORD your God is God; he is the faithful God, keeping his covenant of love to a thousand generations of those who love him and keep his commands.

Deuteronomy 7:9

So if you faithfully obey the commands I am giving you today—to love the LORD your God and to serve him with all your heart and with all your soul—then I will send rain on your land in its season, both autumn and spring rains, so that you may gather in your grain, new wine and oil. I will provide grass in the fields for your cattle, and you will eat and be satisfied.

Deuteronomy 11:13-15

Delight yourself in the LORD and he will give you the desires of your heart.

Psalm 37:4

The LORD watches over all who love him, but all the wicked he will destroy.

Psalm 145:20

I love those who love me, and those who seek me find me.

Proverbs 8:17

Whoever has my commands and obeys them, he is the one who loves me. He who loves me will be loved by my Father, and I too will love him and show myself to him."

John 14:21

No eye has seen, no ear has heard, no mind has conceived what God has prepared for those who love him.

I Corinthians 2:9

Grace to all who love our Lord Jesus Christ with an undying love.

Ephesians 6:24

• Is God the Ultimate Provider for Your Family?
Who cuts a channel for the torrents of rain,
and a path for the thunderstorm,
to water a land where no man lives,
a desert with no one in it, to satisfy

33

a desolate wasteland and make it sprout with grass?
Does the rain have a father?
Who fathers the drops of dew?
From whose womb comes the ice?

Who gives birth to the frost from the heavens
when the waters become hard as stone,
when the surface of the deep is frozen?
Can you bind the beautiful Pleiades?
Can you loose the cords of Orion?
Can you bring forth the constellations in their seasons
or lead out the Bear with its cubs?
Do you know the laws of the heavens?
Can you set up God'sdominion over the earth?
Can you raise your voice to the clouds
and cover yourself with a flood of water?
Do you send the lightning bolts on their way?
Do they report to you, 'Here we are'?
Who endowed the heart with wisdom
or gave understanding to the mind?
Who has the wisdom to count the clouds?
Who can tip over the water jars of the heavens
when the dust becomes hard
and the clods of earth stick together?
Do you hunt the prey for the lioness
and satisfy the hunger of the lions

when they crouch in their dens
or lie in wait in a thicket?
Who provides food for the raven
when its young cry out to God
and wander about for lack of food?

Job 38:25-41

He provides food for those who fear him; he remembers his covenant forever.

Psalm 111:5

You will have plenty to eat, until you are full, and you will praise the name of the LORD your God, who has worked wonders for you; never again will my people be shamed.

Joel 2:26

You care for the land and water it; you enrich it abundantly. The streams of God are filled with water to provide the people with grain, for so you have ordained it.

Psalm 65:9

• Do You Offer Christian Hospitality from Your Home?

I tell you the truth, anyone who gives you a cup of

water in my name because you belong to Christ will certainly not lose his reward.

Mark 9:41

" 'For I was hungry and you gave me something to eat, I was thirsty and you gave me something to drink, I was a stranger and you invited me in, I needed clothes and you clothed me, I was sick and you looked after me, I was in prison and you came to visit me.'. . . "The King will reply, 'I tell you the truth, whatever you did for one of the least of these brothers of mine, you did for me.'

Matthew 25:35-40

It is more blessed to give than to receive.

Acts 20:35b

Share with God's people who are in need. Practice hospitality.

Romans 12:13

Suppose a brother or sister is without clothes and daily food. If one of you says to him, "Go, I wish you well; keep warm and well fed," but does nothing about his physical needs, what good is it?

James 2:15, 16

Offer hospitality to one another without grumbling. Each one should use whatever gift he has received to serve others, faithfully administering God's grace in its various forms.

I Peter 4:9, 10

If anyone has material possessions and sees his brother in need but has no pity on him, how can the love of God be in him?

I John 3:17

Do not forget to entertain strangers, for by so doing some people have entertained angels without knowing it.

Hebrews 13:2

• Do You Maintain High Standards of Sexual Fidelity?

Marriage should be honored by all, and the marriage bed kept pure, for God will judge the adulterer and all the sexually immoral.

Hebrews 13:4

Enjoy life with your wife, whom you love, all the days of this meaningless life that God has given you under the sun—all your meaningless days. For this is your lot in life and in your toilsome labor under the sun.

Ecclesiastes 9:9

In the same way, count yourselves dead to sin but alive to God in Christ Jesus. Therefore do not let sin reign in your mortal body so that you obey its evil desires.

Do not offer the parts of your body to sin, as instruments of wickedness, but rather offer yourselves to God, as those who have been brought from death to life; and offer the parts of your body to him as instruments of righteousness. For sin shall not be your master, because you are not under law, but under grace.

Romans 6:11-14

Flee the evil desires of youth, and pursue righteousness, faith, love and peace, along with those who call on the Lord out of a pure heart.

II Timothy 2:22

Dear friends, I urge you, as aliens and strangers in the world, to abstain from sinful desires, which war against your soul.

I Peter 2:11

"Food for the stomach and the stomach for food"— but God will destroy them both. The body is not meant for sexual immorality, but for the Lord, and the Lord for the body. . . . Do you not know that your bodies are members of Christ himself? Shall I then take the members of Christ and unite them with a prostitute? Never!

I Corinthians 6:13-15

You have heard that it was said, "Do not commit adultery." But I tell you that anyone who looks at a woman lustfully has already committed adultery with her in his heart.

Matthew 5:27, 28

Kids Need to Know Their Parents Are Still in Love

To the married I give this command (not I, but the Lord): A wife must not separate from her husband. But if she does, she must remain unmarried or else

39

be reconciled to her husband. And a husband must not divorce his wife. To the rest I say this (I, not the Lord): If any brother has a wife who is not a believer and she is willing to live with him, he must not divorce her. And if a woman has a husband who is not a believer and he is willing to live with her, she must not divorce him. For the unbelieving husband has been sanctified through his wife, and the unbelieving wife has been sanctified through her believing husband.

Otherwise your children would be unclean, but as it is, they are holy. But if the unbeliever leaves, let him do so. A believing man or woman is not bound in such circumstances; God has called us to live in peace. How do you know, wife, whether

you will save your husband? Or, how do you know, husband, whether you will save your wife?

I Corinthians 7:10-16

• *Husband, Do You Adore Your Wife?*

How beautiful you are, my darling!
Oh, how beautiful!
Your eyes behind your veil are doves.
Your hair is like a flock of goats
descending from Mount Gilead.

Your teeth are like a flock of sheep just shorn,
coming up from the washing.
Each has its twin; not one of them is alone.
Your lips are like a scarlet ribbon;
your mouth is lovely.
Your temples behind your veil
are like the halves of a pomegranate.
Your neck is like the tower of David,
built with elegance;
on it hang a thousand shields,
all of them shields of warriors.
Your two breasts are like two fawns,
like twin fawns of a gazelle
that browse among the lilies.
Until the day breaks and the shadows flee,
I will go to the mountain of myrrh
and to the hill of incense.
All beautiful you are, my darling;
there is no flaw in you.

Song of Songs 4:1-7

She sees that her trading is profitable,
and her lamp does not go out at night.
In her hand she holds the distaff

and grasps the spindle with her fingers.
She opens her arms to the poor
and extends her hands to the needy.
When it snows, she has no fear for her household;
for all of them are clothed in scarlet.
She makes coverings for her bed;
she is clothed in fine linen and purple.
Her husband is respected at the city gate,
where he takes his seat among the elders of the land.
She makes linen garments and sells them,
and supplies the merchants with sashes.
She is clothed with strength and dignity;
she can laugh at the days to come.
She speaks with wisdom,
and faithful instruction is on her tongue.
She watches over the affairs of her household
and does not eat the bread of idleness.
Her children arise and call her blessed;
her husband also, and he praises her:
Many women do noble things,
but you surpass them all.

Proverbs 31:18-29

Submit to one another out of reverence for Christ. . . .
Husbands, love your wives, just as Christ loved the
church and gave himself up for her to make her

holy, cleansing her by the washing with water through the word, and to present her to himself as a radiant church, without stain or wrinkle or any other blemish, but holy and blameless. In this same way, husbands ought to love their wives as their own bodies. He who loves his wife loves himself. After all, no one ever hated his own body, but he feeds and cares for it, just as Christ does the church— for we are members of his body. "For this reason a man will leave his father and mother and be united to his wife, and the two will become one flesh." This is a profound mystery—but I am talking about Christ and the church. However, each one of you also must love his wife as he loves himself.

Ephesians 5:21-33a

Husbands, in the same way be considerate as you live with your wives, and treat them with respect as the weaker partner and as heirs with you of the gracious gift of life, so that nothing will hinder your prayers.

I Peter 3:7

• *Wife, Do You Adore Your Husband?*
My lover is radiant and ruddy,
outstanding among ten thousand.
His head is purest gold;

43

his hair is wavy and black as a raven.
His eyes are like doves by the water streams,
washed in milk, mounted like jewels.
His cheeks are like beds of spice yielding perfume.
His lips are like lilies dripping with myrrh.
His arms are rods of gold set with chrysolite.
His body is like polished ivory
decorated with sapphires.
His legs are pillars of marble
set on bases of pure gold.
His appearance is like Lebanon,
choice as its cedars.
His mouth is sweetness itself; he is altogether lovely.
This is my lover, this my friend,
O daughters of Jerusalem.

Song of Songs 5:10-16

Wives, submit to your husbands as to the Lord. For
the husband is the head of the wife as Christ is the
head of the church, his body, of which he is the Savior. Now as the church submits to Christ, so also
wives should submit to their husbands in everything.

Ephesians 5:22-24

Teach the older women to be reverent in the way
they live, not to be slanderers or addicted to much

wine, but to teach what is good. Then they can train the younger women to love their husbands and children, to be self-controlled and pure, to be busy at home, to be kind, and to be subject to their husbands, so that no one will malign the word of God.

Titus 2:3-5

For Personal Prayer:

Father, You've given me the privilege of being a parent and a home builder. I invite You to be at the very center of our family life. I need Your help and guidance to keep encouraging loving talk and actions in the privacy of our family relationships. Amen.

CHAPTER 3

'How can I build my child's self-esteem?'

The thing I remember about my own childhood," said Jamal, "is that you had to keep producing to get any affection. My folks were great at encouraging me to get good grades, excel in sports, and work hard at a part-time job after school. But I thought I had to keep those things going perfectly in order to keep getting their approval. Maybe that wasn't true, but the fact is, I never really felt their blessing.

"Sure, I want my own children to be 'successful.' But I don't want them thinking they can only get my love when they show me their latest accomplishment."

FOR MEMORY:

Now I commit you to God and to the word of his grace, which can build you up and give you an inheritance among all those who are sanctified.

Acts 20:32

FOR SILENT REFLECTION:

- *How was I "built up" or "cut down" as a child?*

- *If I could ask my own parents for a "blessing," what would I want them to do or say?*

- *In what ways have I let my child know that he or she is loved and valued apart from accomplishments?*

- *To what level do my kids sense that I love them unconditionally?*

Bless Your Children, Face-to-Face:

Blessed are you (_____Your Child's Name_____),
when you do not walk in the counsel of the wicked
or stand in the way of sinners or sit in the seat of mockers.
But your delight is in the law of the LORD,
and on his law may you meditate day and night.
Then you will be like a tree planted by streams of
water,
which yields its fruit in season
and whose leaf does not wither.
Whatever you do will prosper.
Not so the wicked!
They are like chaff that the wind blows away.
Therefore the wicked will not stand in the judgment,
nor sinners in the assembly of the righteous.
For the LORD watches over the way of the righteous,
but the way of the wicked will perish.

Psalm 1:1-6 (paraphrased)

My son/daughter, (_____Name_____),
if you accept my words
and store up my commands within you,
turning your ear to wisdom
and applying your heart to understanding,
and if you call out for insight

49

and cry aloud for understanding,
and if you look for it as for silver
and search for it as for hidden treasure,
then you will understand the fear of the LORD
and find the knowledge of God.
For the LORD gives wisdom,
and from his mouth come knowledge and understanding.
He holds victory in store for the upright,
he is a shield to those whose walk is blameless,
for he guards the course of the just
and protects the way of his faithful ones.

Proverbs 2:1-8

Trust in the LORD with all your heart, (___Name___),
and lean not on your own understanding;
in all your ways acknowledge him,
and he will make your paths straight.

Proverbs 3:5, 6

I pray that out of his glorious riches [God] may
strengthen you, (___Name___), with power
through his Spirit in your inner being, so that Christ
may dwell in your hearts through faith. And I pray
that you, being rooted and established in love, may
have power, together with all the saints, to grasp
how wide and long and high and deep is the love of

Christ, and to know this love that surpasses knowledge—that you may be filled to the measure of all the fullness of God.

Ephesians 3:16-19

Tell of God's Blessings, Too:

Moses said to God, "Who am I, that I should go to Pharaoh and bring the Israelites out of Egypt?"

Exodus 3:11

Mephibosheth bowed down and said, "What is your servant, that you should notice a dead dog like me?"

II Samuel 9:8

• Honored In Creation

So God created man in his own image, in the image of God he created him; male and female he created them. God blessed them and said to them, "Be fruitful and increase in number; fill the earth and subdue it. Rule over the fish of the sea and the birds of the air and over every living creature that moves on the ground." Then God said, "I give you every seed-bearing plant on the face of the whole earth and every tree that has fruit with seed in it. They will be yours for food. And to all the beasts of the earth and all the birds of the air and all the creatures that move

51

on the ground—everything that has the breath of life in it—I give every green plant for food." And it was so.

God saw all that he had made, and it was very good.

Genesis 1:27-31a

I praise you because I am fearfully and wonderfully made;
your works are wonderful,
I know that full well.
My frame was not hidden from you
when I was made in the secret place.
When I was woven together
in the depths of the earth,
your eyes saw my unformed body.
All the days ordained for me
were written in your book
before one of them came to be.

Psalm 139:14-16

What is man that you are mindful of him,
the son of man that you care for him?
You made him a little lower than the heavenly beings
and crowned him with glory and honor.
You made him ruler over the works of your hands;
you put everything under his feet:

all flocks and herds, and the beasts of the field,
the birds of the air, and the fish of the sea,
all that swim the paths of the seas.
O LORD, our Lord, how majestic is your name in all the
earth!

Psalm 8:4-9

• *Given a Mission in the Kingdom*

Therefore go and make disciples of all nations, baptizing them in the name of the Father and of the Son and of the Holy Spirit, and teaching them to obey everything I have commanded you. And surely I am with you always, to the very end of the age.

Matthew 28:19, 20

Therefore, if anyone is in Christ, he is a new creation; the old has gone, the new has come! All this is from God, who reconciled us to himself through Christ and gave us the ministry of reconciliation: that God was reconciling the world to himself in Christ, not counting men's sins against them. And he has committed to us the message of reconciliation. We are therefore Christ's ambassadors, as though God were making his appeal through us. We implore you on Christ's behalf: Be reconciled to God.

II Corinthians 5:17-20

For we are God's workmanship, created in Christ
Jesus to do good works, which God prepared in
advance for us to do.

Ephesians 2:10

And we pray this in order that you may live a life
worthy of the Lord and may please him in every
way: bearing fruit in every good work, growing in
the knowledge of God, being strengthened with all
power according to his glorious might so that you
may have great endurance and patience, and joyful-
ly giving thanks to the Father, who has qualified you
to share in the inheritance of the saints in the kingdom of light.

Colossians 1:10-12

• Blameless in God's Sight

To him who is able to keep you from falling and to
present you before his glorious presence without
fault and with great joy—to the only God our Savior
be glory, majesty, power and authority, through Jesus
Christ our Lord, before all ages, now and forevermore! Amen.

Jude 1:24, 25

The LORD has dealt with me according to my righteousness; according to the cleanness of my hands he

has rewarded me. For I have kept the ways of the LORD; I have not done evil by turning from my God. All his laws are before me; I have not turned away from his decrees. I have been blameless before him and have kept myself from sin. The LORD has rewarded me according to my righteousness, according to my cleanness in his sight. To the faithful you show yourself faithful, to the blameless you show yourself blameless, to the pure you show yourself pure.

II Samuel 22:21-27a

Praise be to the LORD,
for he showed his wonderful love to me
when I was in a besieged city.
In my alarm I said, "I am cut off from your sight!"
Yet you heard my cry for mercy
when I called to you for help.
Love the LORD, all his saints!
The LORD preserves the faithful,
but the proud he pays back in full.
Be strong and take heart,
all you who hope in the LORD.

Psalm 31:21-24

But Jesus went to the Mount of Olives. At dawn he appeared again in the temple courts, where all the people gathered around him, and he sat down to teach them. The teachers of the law and the Pharisees brought in a woman caught in adultery. They made her stand before the group and said to Jesus, "Teacher, this woman was caught in the act of adultery.

"In the Law Moses commanded us to stone such women. Now what do you say?" They were using this question as a trap, in order to have a basis for accusing him. But Jesus bent down and started to write on the ground with his finger. When they kept on questioning him, he straightened up and said to them, "If any one of you is without sin, let him be the first to throw a stone at her."

Again he stooped down and wrote on the ground. At this, those who heard began to go away one at a time, the older ones first, until only Jesus was left, with the woman still standing there. Jesus straightened up and asked her, "Woman, where are they? Has no one condemned you?"

"No one, sir," she said. "Then neither do I condemn you," Jesus declared. "Go now and leave your life of sin."

John 8:1-11

Therefore, there is now no condemnation for those who are in Christ Jesus, because through Christ Jesus the law of the Spirit of life set me free from the law of sin and death. For what the law was powerless to do in that it was weakened by the sinful nature, God did by sending his own Son in the likeness of sinful man to be a sin offering. And so he condemned sin in sinful man, in order that the righteous requirements of the law might be fully met in us, who do not live according to the sinful nature but according to the Spirit.

Romans 8:1-4

This then is how we know that we belong to the truth, and how we set our hearts at rest in his presence whenever our hearts condemn us. For God is greater than our hearts, and he knows everything. Dear friends, if our hearts do not condemn us, we have confidence before God.

I John 3:19-21

May God himself, the God of peace, sanctify you through and through. May your whole spirit, soul and body be kept blameless at the coming of our Lord Jesus Christ. The one who calls you is faithful and he will do it.

I Thessalonians 5:23, 24

• *Created for Blessing*

If you then, though you are evil, know how to give good gifts to your children, how much more will

your Father in heaven give the Holy Spirit to those
who ask him!"

Luke 11:13

The LORD your God is bringing you into a good
land—a land with streams and pools of water, with
springs flowing in the valleys and hills; a land with
wheat and barley, vines and fig trees, pomegranates,
olive oil and honey; a land where bread will not be
scarce and you will lack nothing; a land where the
rocks are iron and you can dig copper out of the
hills. When you have eaten and are satisfied, praise
the LORD your God for the good land he has given
you. . . . .You may say to yourself, "My power and
the strength of my hands have produced this wealth
for me." But remember the LORD your God, for it is
he who gives you the ability to produce wealth, and
so confirms his covenant, which he swore to your
forefathers, as it is today.

Deuteronomy 8: 7-18

For he will command his angels concerning you
to guard you in all your ways;
they will lift you up in their hands,
so that you will not strike your foot against a stone.
You will tread upon the lion and the cobra;
you will trample the great lion and the serpent.

58

"Because he loves me," says the LORD,
"I will rescue him; I will protect him,
for he acknowledges my name.
He will call upon me, and I will answer him;
I will be with him in trouble,
I will deliver him and honor him.
With long life will I satisfy him
and show him my salvation."

Psalm 91:11-16

Be glad, O people of Zion,
rejoice in the LORD your God,
for he has given you the autumn rains in righteousness.
He sends you abundant showers,
both autumn and spring rains, as before.
The threshing floors will be filled with grain;
the vats will overflow with new wine and oil.

Joel 2:23, 24

And my God will meet all your needs according to
his glorious riches in Christ Jesus.

Philippians 4:19

Then you will call, and the LORD will answer; you
will cry for help, and he will say: Here am I. . . . .
The LORD will guide you always;
he will satisfy your needs in a sun-scorched land

and will strengthen your frame.
You will be like a well-watered garden,
like a spring whose waters never fail.

Isaiah 58:9, 11

They will come and shout for joy on the heights of
Zion;
they will rejoice in the bounty of the LORD—
the grain, the new wine and the oil,
the young of the flocks and herds.
They will be like a well-watered garden,
and they will sorrow no more.
Then maidens will dance and be glad,
young men and old as well.
I will turn their mourning into gladness;
I will give them comfort and joy instead of sorrow.
I will satisfy the priests with abundance,
and my people will be filled with my bounty,"
declares the LORD.

Jeremiah 31:12-14

And afterward, I will pour out my Spirit on all people.
Your sons and daughters will prophesy,
your old men will dream dreams,
your young men will see visions.
Even on my servants, both men and women,

I will pour out my Spirit in those days.
I will show wonders in the heavens and on the earth,
blood and fire and billows of smoke.
The sun will be turned to darkness
and the moon to blood before the coming of the great and dreadful day of the LORD.
And everyone who calls on the name of the LORD will be saved;
for on Mount Zion and in Jerusalem
there will be deliverance, as the LORD has said,
among the survivors whom the LORD calls.

Joel 2:28-32

And I will ask the Father, and he will give you another Counselor to be with you forever—Spirit of truth. The world cannot accept him, because it neither sees him nor knows him. But you know him, for he lives with you and will be in you.

But the Counselor, the Holy Spirit, whom the Father will send in my name, will teach you all things and will remind you of everything I have said to you. Peace I leave with you; my peace I give you. I do not give to you as the world gives. Do not let your hearts be troubled and do not be afraid.

John 14:16, 17, 26, 27

Now I commit you to God and to the word of his grace, which can build you up and give you an inheritance among all those who are sanctified.

Acts 20:32

To him who is able to keep you from falling and to present you before his glorious presence without fault and with great joy—to the only God our Savior be glory, majesty, power and authority, through Jesus Christ our Lord, before all ages, now and forevermore! Amen.

Jude 1:24, 25

• Heirs to a Crown

Everyone who competes in the games goes into strict training. They do it to get a crown that will not last; but we do it to get a crown that will last forever.

I Corinthians 9:25

Now there is in store for me the crown of righteousness, which the Lord, the righteous Judge, will award to me on that day—and not only to me, but also to all who have longed for his appearing.

II Timothy 4:8

Blessed is the man who perseveres under trial, because when he has stood the test, he will receive the crown of life that God has promised to those who love him.

James 1:12

And when the Chief Shepherd appears, you will receive the crown of glory that will never fade away.

I Peter 5:4

Do not be afraid of what you are about to suffer. I tell you, the devil will put some of you in prison to test you, and you will suffer persecution for ten days. Be faithful, even to the point of death, and I will give you the crown of life.

Revelation 2:10

FOR PERSONAL PRAYER:

Lord, thank You for the eternal basis of my self-esteem: that I am Your creation, and that You have adopted me as Your child. I want my children to know that they, too, are Yours, accepted by You unconditionally. Help me come as close as possible to conveying that same kind of unconditional acceptance to my children every day. Amen.

CHAPTER 4

'Why am I always yelling at the kids?'

I've got a baby on the way and I think I'm more prepared for this one, in terms of understanding discipline," said Charlene. "But I hope I'm not too late with my other kids in realizing that discipline takes a lot more time and effort than just handing out punishments.

"I can see now that the whole idea is to be teaching and training from the very beginning. Then discipline is not a matter of yelling every time kids slip up. It's giving them the knowledge and skills they need to start correcting their own behavior."

FOR MEMORY:

These commandments that I give you today are to be upon your hearts. Impress them on your children. Talk about them when you sit at home and when you walk along the road, when you lie down and when you get up.

Deuteronomy 6:6, 7

FOR SILENT REFLECTION:

- *When I last yelled or lashed out at my children, what did I really teach them?*

- *How can I begin to undo past mistakes in disciplining my kids?*

- *What success can I recall in teaching and training my children?*

- *What informal means of instruction would help my children better recognize God's will in their lives?*

Teach and Train Your Children

Be careful, and watch yourselves closely so that you do not forget the things your eyes have seen or let them slip from your heart as long as you live. Teach them to your children and to their children after them. Remember the day you stood before the LORD your God at Horeb, when he said to me, "Assemble the people before me to hear my words so that they may learn to revere me as long as they live in the land and may teach them to their children."

Deuteronomy 4:9, 10

These commandments that I give you today are to be upon your hearts. Impress them on your children. Talk about them when you sit at home and when you walk along the road, when you lie down and when you get up. Tie them as symbols on your hands and bind them on your foreheads. Write them on the doorframes of your houses and on your gates.

Deuteronomy 6:6-9

Teach them to your children, talking about them when you sit at home and when you walk along the road, when you lie down and when you get up.

Deuteronomy 11:19

I will open my mouth in parables,
I will utter hidden things, things from of old—
what we have heard and known,
what our fathers have told us.
We will not hide them from their children;
we will tell the next generation
the praiseworthy deeds of the LORD,
his power, and the wonders he has done.

Psalm 78:2-4

• Help Them Accept Your Correction

Honor your father and your mother, as the LORD your God has commanded you, so that you may live long and that it may go well with you in the land the LORD your God is giving you.

Deuteronomy 5:16

Do not forsake your mother's teaching.

Proverbs 6:20b

Children, obey your parents in everything, for this pleases the Lord.

Colossians 3:20

My son, if your heart is wise, then my heart will be glad; my inmost being will rejoice when your lips speak what is right. . . . Listen to your father, who gave you life, and do not despise your mother when she is old. . . . The father of a righteous man has great joy; he who has a wise son delights in him. May your father and mother be glad; may she who gave you birth rejoice! My son, give me your heart and let your eyes keep to my ways.

Proverbs 23:15-26

•*Accept God's Correction In Your Life, Too*

My son, do not make light of the Lord's discipline, and do not lose heart when he rebukes you, because the Lord disciplines those he loves, and he punishes everyone he accepts as a son.

Endure hardship as discipline; God is treating you as sons. For what son is not disciplined by his father? If you are not disciplined (and everyone undergoes discipline), then you are illegitimate children and not true sons. Moreover, we have all had human fathers who disciplined us and we respected them for it. How much more should we submit to the Father of our spirits and live! Our fathers disciplined us for a little while as they thought best; but God disciplines us for our good, that we may share in his holiness. No discipline seems pleasant at the time, but painful. Later on,

however, it produces a harvest of righteousness and
peace for those who have been trained by it.

Hebrews 12:5b-11

Blessed is the man whom God corrects;
so do not despise the discipline of the Almighty.
For he wounds, but he also binds up;
he injures, but his hands also heal.
From six calamities he will rescue you;
in seven no harm will befall you.
In famine he will ransom you from death,
and in battle from the stroke of the sword.
You will be protected from the lash of the tongue,
and need not fear when destruction comes.
You will laugh at destruction and famine,
and need not fear the beasts of the earth.
For you will have a covenant with the stones of the field,
and the wild animals will be at peace with you.
You will know that your tent is secure;
you will take stock of your property and find nothing
missing.
You will know that your children will be many,
and your descendants like the grass of the earth.
You will come to the grave in full vigor,
like sheaves gathered in season.

Job 5:17-26

• Help Them Learn to Persevere

He who loves pleasure will become poor; whoever loves wine and oil will never be rich.

Proverbs 21:17

But mark this: There will be terrible times in the last days. People will be lovers of themselves, lovers of money, boastful, proud, abusive, disobedient to their parents, ungrateful, unholy, without love, unforgiving, slanderous, without self-control, brutal, not lovers of the good, treacherous, rash, conceited, lovers of pleasure rather than lovers of God.

II Timothy 3:1-4

Therefore, prepare your minds for action; be self-controlled; set your hope fully on the grace to be given you when Jesus Christ is revealed. As obedient children, do not conform to the evil desires you had when you lived in ignorance. But just as he who called you is holy, so be holy in all you do; for it is written: "Be holy, because I am holy."

I Peter 1:13-16

Anyone who does not carry his cross and follow me cannot be my disciple. Suppose one of you wants to build a tower. Will he not first sit down and estimate the cost to see if he has enough money to complete it? For if he lays the foundation and is not able to finish it, everyone who sees it will ridicule him, saying, "This fellow began to build and was not able to finish." Or suppose a king is about to go to war against another king.

Will he not first sit down and consider whether he is able with ten thousand men to oppose the one coming against him with twenty thousand? If he is not able, he will send a delegation while the other is still a long way off and will ask for terms of peace. In the same way, any of you who does not give up everything he has cannot be my disciple.

Salt is good, but if it loses its saltiness, how can it be made salty again? It is fit neither for the soil nor for the manure pile; it is thrown out. He who has ears to hear, let him hear."

Luke 14:27-35

That is why I am suffering as I am. Yet I am not ashamed, because I know whom I have believed, and am convinced that he is able to guard what I have entrusted to him for that day.

II Timothy 1:12

• Help Them Resist Their Temptations

What shall we say, then? Shall we go on sinning so that grace may increase? By no means! We died to sin; how can we live in it any longer? Or don't you know that all of us who were baptized into Christ Jesus were baptized into his death? We were therefore buried with him through baptism into death in order that, just as Christ was raised from the dead through the glory of the Father, we too may live a new life. If we have been united with him like this in his death, we will certainly also be united with him in his resurrection. For we know that our old self was crucified with him so that the body of sin might be done away with, that we should no longer be slaves to sin—because anyone who has died has been freed from sin. . . . In the same way, count yourselves dead to sin but alive to God in Christ Jesus. Therefore do not let sin reign in your mortal body so that you obey its evil desires.

Romans 6:1-12

No temptation has seized you except what is common to man. And God is faithful; he will not let you be tempted beyond what you can bear. But when you are tempted, he will also provide a way out so that you can stand up under it.

I Corinthians 10:13

Finally, be strong in the Lord and in his mighty power. Put on the full armor of God so that you can take your stand against the devil's schemes. For our struggle is not against flesh and blood, but against the rulers, against the authorities, against the powers of this dark world and against the spiritual forces of evil in the heavenly realms. Therefore put on the full armor of God, so that when the day of evil comes, you may be able to stand your ground, and after you have done everything, to stand. Stand firm then, with the belt of truth buckled around your waist, with the breastplate of righteousness in place, and with your feet fitted with the readiness that comes from the gospel of peace. In addition to all this, take up the shield of faith, with which you can extinguish all the flaming arrows of the evil one. Take the helmet of salvation and the sword of the Spirit, which is the word of God. And pray in the Spirit on all occasions with all kinds of prayers and requests. With this in mind, be alert and always keep on praying for all the saints.

Ephesians 6:10-18

But the Lord is faithful, and he will strengthen and protect you from the evil one.

II Thessalonians 3:3

Be self-controlled and alert. Your enemy the devil prowls around like a roaring lion looking for someone to devour. Resist him, standing firm in the faith, because you know that your brothers throughout the world are undergoing the same kind of sufferings. And the God of all grace, who called you to his eternal glory in Christ, after you have suffered a little while, will himself restore you and make you strong, firm and steadfast.

I Peter 5:8-10

• Help Them Develop Good Work Habits

I went past the field of the sluggard, past the vineyard of the man who lacks judgment; thorns had come up everywhere, the ground was covered with weeds, and the stone wall was in ruins. I applied my heart to what I observed and learned a lesson from what I saw: A little sleep, a little slumber, a little folding of the hands to rest—and poverty will come on you like a bandit and scarcity like an armed man.

Proverbs 24:30-34

Mind your own business and work with your hands, just as we told you, so that your daily life may win the respect of outsiders and so that you will not be dependent on anybody.

I Thessalonians 4:11b, 12

75

For even when we were with you, we gave you this rule: "If a man will not work, he shall not eat." We hear that some among you are idle. They are not busy; they are busybodies. Such people we command and urge in the Lord Jesus Christ to settle down and earn the bread they eat.

II Thessalonians 3:10-12

Do you not know that in a race all the runners run, but only one gets the prize? Run in such a way as to get the prize. Everyone who competes in the games goes into strict training. They do it to get a crown that will not last; but we do it to get a crown that will last forever. Therefore I do not run like a man running aimlessly; I do not fight like a man beating the air. No, I beat my body and make it my slave so that after I have preached to others, I myself will not be disqualified for the prize.

I Corinthians 9:24-27

Do not merely listen to the word, and so deceive yourselves. Do what it says. Anyone who listens to the word but does not do what it says is like a man who looks at his face in a mirror and, after looking at himself, goes away and immediately forgets what he looks like. But the man who looks intently into the perfect law that gives freedom, and continues to do this, not forgetting what he has heard, but doing it—he will be blessed in what he does. If anyone considers himself religious and yet does not keep a tight rein on his tongue, he deceives himself and his religion is worthless. Religion that God our Father accepts as pure and faultless is this: to look after orphans and widows in their distress and to keep oneself from being polluted by the world.

James 1:22-27

• Help Them Develop Self-Discipline and Trustworthiness

Then Jesus said to his disciples, "If anyone would come after me, he must deny himself and take up his cross and follow me. For whoever wants to save his life will lose it, but whoever loses his life for me will find it. What good will it be for a man if he gains the whole world, yet forfeits his soul? Or what can a man give in exchange for his soul?

Matthew 16:24-26

Therefore, brothers, we have an obligation—but it is not to the sinful nature, to live according to it. For if you live according to the sinful nature, you will die; but if by the Spirit you put to death the misdeeds of the body, you will live.

Romans 8:12, 13

Those who belong to Christ Jesus have crucified the sinful nature with its passions and desires.

Galatians 5:24

For the grace of God that brings salvation has appeared to all men. It teaches us to say "No" to ungodliness and worldly passions, and to live self-controlled, upright and godly lives in this present age.

Titus 2:11, 12

A gossip betrays a confidence, but a trustworthy man keeps a secret.

Proverbs 11:13

Teach slaves to be subject to their masters in everything, to try to please them, not to talk back to them, and not to steal from them, but to show that they can be fully trusted, so that in every way they will make the teaching about God our Savior attractive.

Titus 2:9, 10

• Help Them Get Along with One Another

Let's not have any quarreling between you and me, or between your herdsmen and mine, for we are brothers.

Genesis 13:8b

I appeal to you, brothers, in the name of our Lord Jesus Christ, that all of you agree with one another so that there may be no divisions among you and that you may be perfectly united in mind and thought.

I Corinthians 1:10

Finally, all of you, live in harmony with one another; be sympathetic, love as brothers, be compassionate and humble.

I Peter 3:8

Let us therefore make every effort to do what leads to peace and to mutual edification.

Romans 14:19

May the God who gives endurance and encouragement give you a spirit of unity among yourselves as you follow Christ Jesus, so that with one heart and mouth you may glorify the God and Father of our Lord Jesus Christ.

Romans 15:5, 6

Use Punishment Wisely

Discipline your son, and he will give you peace; he will bring delight to your soul.

Proverbs 29:17

He who spares the rod hates his son, but he who loves him is careful to discipline him.

Proverbs 13:24

Folly is bound up in the heart of a child, but the rod of discipline will drive it far from him.

Proverbs 22:15

Do not withhold discipline from a child; if you punish him with the rod, he will not die.

Proverbs 23:13

If you, then, though you are evil, know how to give good gifts to your children, how much more will your Father in heaven give good gifts to those who ask him!

Matthew 7:11

FOR PERSONAL PRAYER:

Lord, I find it easier to yell and punish than to instruct and train my children. But give me the patience and perseverance to fight against taking the easy way out. Convince me, deep inside, that my time and energy could not be given to a worthier cause. Amen.

CHAPTER 5

'What are the lasting values to give my children?'

*B*ut, Mom, everybody else is doing it!

"How many times have I heard that from my two teens in the last month? It seems to be their standard argument for everything," says Karen. "Of course, I, too, used to try that approach on my own parents. But my kids know it's not going to work, even though they keep testing my resolve."

FOR MEMORY:

Do not conform any longer to the pattern of this world, but be transformed by the renewing of your mind. Then you will be able to test and approve what God's will is—his good, pleasing and perfect will.

Romans 12:2

FOR SILENT REFLECTION:

- *What values and character traits am I seeking to build into my own life right now?*

- *What character traits do I see forming in my children?*

- *How do I react when I find society calling into question the values of my Christian family?*

- *How can I respond positively, rather than defensively, in order to display the wisdom of God's values?*

Biblical Values to Teach Your Children

• *Compassion*

As a father has compassion on his children, so the LORD has compassion on those who fear him.

Psalm 103:13

I will plant her for myself in the land; I will show my love to the one I called "Not my loved one." I will say to those called "Not my people," "You are my people"; and they will say, "You are my God."

Hosea 2:23

Be merciful to those who doubt; snatch others from the fire and save them; to others show mercy, mixed with fear—hating even the clothing stained by corrupted flesh.

Jude 22, 23

• *Faith*

Then Caleb silenced the people before Moses and said, "We should go up and take possession of the land, for we can certainly do it."

-Numbers 13:30

Even though I walk through the valley of the shadow

of death, I will fear no evil, for you are with me; your rod and your staff, they comfort me.

Psalm 23: 4

Say to those with fearful hearts, "Be strong, do not fear; your God will come, he will come with vengeance; with divine retribution he will come to save you."

Isaiah 35: 4

I tell you the truth, if you have faith as small as a mustard seed, you can say to this mountain, 'Move from here to there' and it will move. Nothing will be impossible for you."

Matthew 17:20b

For nothing is impossible with God.

Luke 1:37

Without faith it is impossible to please God, because anyone who comes to him must believe that he exists and that he rewards those who earnestly seek him.

Hebrews 11:6

For everyone born of God overcomes the world. This is the victory that has overcome the world, even our faith. . . . This is the confidence we have in approaching God: that if we ask anything according to his will, he hears us. And if we know that he hears us—whatever we ask—we know that we have what we asked of him.

I John 5:4-15

• *Wisdom*

Surely you desire truth in the inner parts; you teach me wisdom in the inmost place.

Psalm 51:6

To the man who pleases him, God gives wisdom, knowledge and happiness, but to the sinner he gives the task of gathering and storing up wealth to hand it over to the one who pleases God.

Ecclesiastes 2:26a

For God, who said, "Let light shine out of darkness," made his light shine in our hearts to give us the light of the knowledge of the glory of God in the face of Christ.

II Corinthians 4:6

If any of you lacks wisdom, he should ask God, who gives generously to all without finding fault, and it will be given to him.

James 1:5

87

We know also that the Son of God has come and has given us understanding, so that we may know him who is true. And we are in him who is true—even in his Son Jesus Christ. He is the true God and eternal life.

I John 5:20

• *Obedience to God*

Love the LORD your God with all your heart and with all your soul and with all your strength.

Deuteronomy 6:5

If they obey and serve him, they will spend the rest of their days in prosperity and their years in contentment.

Job 36:11

May the words of my mouth and the meditation of my heart be pleasing in your sight, O LORD, my Rock and my Redeemer.

Psalm 19:14

No one can serve two masters. Either he will hate the one and love the other, or he will be devoted to the one and despise the other. You cannot serve both God and Money.

Matthew 6:24

We know that we have come to know him if we obey his commands.

I John 2:3

So whether you eat or drink or whatever you do, do it all for the glory of God.

I Corinthians 10:31

•*Forgiveness*

Love your enemies and pray for those who persecute you, that you may be sons of your Father in heaven. He causes his sun to rise on the evil and the good, and sends rain on the righteous and the unrighteous.

Matthew 5:44, 45

For if you forgive men when they sin against you, your heavenly Father will also forgive you.

Matthew 6:14

And when you stand praying, if you hold anything against anyone, forgive him, so that your Father in heaven may forgive you your sins.

Mark 11:25

If your enemy is hungry, feed him; if he is thirsty, give him something to drink. In doing this, you will heap burning coals on his head.

Romans 12:20

•*Honesty*

You must have accurate and honest weights and measures, so that you may live long in the land the LORD your God is giving you. For the LORD your God detests anyone who does these things, anyone who deals dishonestly.

Deuteronomy 25:15, 16

Keep me from deceitful ways;
be gracious to me through your law.
I have chosen the way of truth;
I have set my heart on your laws.
I hold fast to your statutes, O LORD;
do not let me be put to shame.
I run in the path of your commands,
for you have set my heart free.
Teach me, O LORD, to follow your decrees;
then I will keep them to the end.

Psalm 119:29-33

Do not lie to each other, since you have taken off your old self with its practices and have put on the new self, which is being renewed in knowledge in the image of its Creator.

Colossians 3:9, 10

• *Humility*

He mocks proud mockers but gives grace to the humble.

Proverbs 3:34

The fear of the LORD teaches a man wisdom, and humility comes before honor.

Proverbs 15:33

Better to be lowly in spirit and among the oppressed than to share plunder with the proud.

Proverbs 16:19

Therefore, whoever humbles himself like this child is the greatest in the kingdom of heaven.

Matthew 18:4

But he gives us more grace. That is why Scripture says: "God opposes the proud but gives grace to the humble."

James 4:6

Humble yourselves, therefore, under God's mighty hand, that he may lift you up in due time.

I Peter 5:6

• Peacefulness

I will listen to what God the LORD will say; he promises peace to his people, his saints—but let them not return to folly.

Psalm 85:8

The fruit of righteousness will be peace; the effect of righteousness will be quietness and confidence forever.

Isaiah 32:17

Peace I leave with you; my peace I give you. I do not give to you as the world gives. Do not let your hearts be troubled and do not be afraid.

John 14:27

Let the peace of Christ rule in your hearts, since as members of one body you were called to peace. And be thankful.

Colossians 3:15

Now may the Lord of peace himself give you peace at all times and in every way. The Lord be with all of you.

II Thessalonians 3:16

•Thoughtfulness

In everything, do to others what you would have them do to you, for this sums up the Law and the Prophets.

Matthew 7:12

I tell you the truth, whatever you did for one of the least of these brothers of mine, you did for me.

Matthew 25:40b

Love your enemies, do good to those who hate you.

Luke 6:27b

And now these three remain: faith, hope and love. But the greatest of these is love.

I Corinthians 13:13

•Happiness

The crowd joined in the attack against Paul and Silas, and the magistrates ordered them to be stripped and beaten.

After they had been severely flogged, they were thrown into prison, and the jailer was commanded to guard them carefully. Upon receiving such orders, he put them in the inner cell and fastened their feet in the stocks. About midnight Paul and Silas were praying and singing hymns to God . . . .

Acts 16:22-25a

The LORD has done great things for us, and we are filled with joy.

Psalm 126:3

A happy heart makes the face cheerful, but heartache crushes the spirit.

Proverbs 15:13

A cheerful heart is good medicine, but a crushed spirit dries up the bones.

Proverbs 17:22

I know that there is nothing better for men than to be happy and do good while they live.

Ecclesiastes 3:12

Biblical Values Stand Out in Our Society

Do not conform any longer to the pattern of this world, but be transformed by the renewing of your mind. Then you will be able to test and approve what God's will is—his good, pleasing and perfect will.

Romans 12:2

Since, then, you have been raised with Christ, set your hearts on things above, where Christ is seated at the right hand of God. Set your minds on things above, not on earthly things. For you died, and your life is now hidden with Christ in God. When Christ, who is your life, appears, then you also will appear with him in glory. Put to death, therefore, whatever belongs to your earthly nature: sexual immorality, impurity, lust, evil desires and greed, which is idolatry. Because of these, the wrath of God is coming.

Colossians 3:1-6

Do not love the world or anything in the world. If anyone loves the world, the love of the Father is not in him. For everything in the world—the cravings of sinful man, the lust of his eyes and the boasting of what he has and does—comes not from the Father but from the world. The world and its desires pass away, but the man who does the will of God lives forever.

I John 2:15-17

For everyone born of God overcomes the world. This is the victory that has overcome the world, even our faith. Who is it that overcomes the world? Only he who believes that Jesus is the Son of God.

I John 5:4, 5

Therefore, prepare your minds for action; be self-controlled; set your hope fully on the grace to be given you when Jesus Christ is revealed.

I Peter 1:13

Prepare for Opposition to Your Family's Values

Then Jesus was led by the Spirit into the desert to be tempted by the devil. After fasting forty days and forty nights, he was hungry. The tempter came to him and said, "If you are the Son of God, tell these stones to become bread." Jesus answered, "It is written: 'Man does not live on bread alone, but on every word that comes from the mouth of God.'" Then the devil took him to the holy city and had him stand on the highest point of the temple. "If you are the Son of God," he said, "throw yourself down. For it is written: " 'He will command his angels concerning you, and they will lift you up in their hands, so that you will not strike your foot against a stone.' " Jesus answered him, "It is also written: 'Do not put the Lord your God to the test.' " Again, the devil took him to a very high mountain and showed him all the kingdoms of the world and their splendor. "All this I will give you," he said, "if you will bow down and worship me." Jesus said to him, "Away from me, Satan! For it is written: 'Worship the Lord your God, and serve him only.' " Then the devil left him, and angels came and attended him.

Matthew 4:1-11

If the world hates you, keep in mind that it hated me first. If you belonged to the world, it would love you as its own. As it is, you do not belong to the world, but I have chosen you out of the world. That is why the world hates you."

John 15:18, 19

If you are insulted because of the name of Christ, you are blessed, for the Spirit of glory and of God rests on you. If you suffer, it should not be as a murderer or thief or any other kind of criminal, or even as a meddler. However, if you suffer as a Christian, do not be ashamed, but praise God that you bear that name.

I Peter 4:14, 15

FOR PERSONAL PRAYER:

Heavenly Father, Your values cut across the grain of so much that I see on television and in our society. Give me the courage to confront these values without judging others. May my children see the wisdom and beauty of the plan for human life that Your eternal values represent. Amen.

CHAPTER 6

'What do I do when I feel frustrated with my parenting responsibilities?'

Sometimes I feel like shutting everything out," said Dave. "I'm so tired when I get home from work that I just want to sit on the couch and stare at the TV for a while. Yet, it's just at this point in my day when Linda looks forward to me 'taking over' with the kids. She's been with them all day and wants some relief.

"I never thought you could get burned out on parenting. But with three little kids and very little time, I don't see how it can be avoided."

FOR MEMORY:

Let us not become weary in doing good, for at the proper time we will reap a harvest if we do not give up.

Galatians 6:9

FOR SILENT REFLECTION:

- *How much of my emotional energy is being drained by people and activities that are not true priorities for me?*

- *In what ways could I simplify my days in order to free up more time for quality parenting?*

- *Can I accept frustration as a call to rely more on God's strength?*

- *In practical terms, what would more dependence on God mean for me?*

Beware Parental Burnout

Be merciful to me, LORD, for I am faint; O LORD, heal me, for my bones are in agony.

Psalm 6:2

Show me, O LORD, my life's end
and the number of my days;
let me know how fleeting is my life.
You have made my days a mere handbreadth;
the span of my years is as nothing before you.
Each man's life is but a breath.

Psalm 39:4, 5

My knees give way from fasting; my body is thin and gaunt.

Psalm 109:24

All men are like grass, and all their glory is like the flowers of the field.

Isaiah 40:6b

But God chose the foolish things of the world to shame the wise; God chose the weak things of the world to shame the strong.

I Corinthians 1:27

That is why, for Christ's sake, I delight in weaknesses, in insults, in hardships, in persecutions, in difficulties. For when I am weak, then I am strong.

II Corinthians 12:10

I lift up my eyes to the hills—
where does my help come from?
My help comes from the LORD,
the Maker of heaven and earth.
He will not let your foot slip—
he who watches over you will not slumber;
indeed, he who watches over Israel
will neither slumber nor sleep.
The LORD watches over you—
the LORD is your shade at your right hand;
the sun will not harm you by day,
nor the moon by night.
The LORD will keep you from all harm—
he will watch over your life;
the LORD will watch over your coming and going
both now and forevermore.

Psalm 121:1-8

Give God Your Fears

Be strong and courageous. Do not be afraid or terrified because of them, for the LORD your God goes with you; he will never leave you nor forsake you.

Deuteronomy 31:6

Have I not commanded you? Be strong and courageous. Do not be terrified; do not be discouraged, for the LORD your God will be with you wherever you go.

Joshua 1:9

Though an army besiege me, my heart will not fear; though war break out against me, even then will I be confident.

Psalm 27:3

Therefore we will not fear, though the earth give way and the mountains fall into the heart of the sea.

Psalm 46:2

Whoever listens to me will live in safety and be at ease, without fear of harm.

Proverbs 1:33

Indeed, the very hairs of your head are all numbered. Don't be afraid; you are worth more than many sparrows.

Luke 12:7

Do not be afraid, little flock, for your Father has been pleased to give you the kingdom.

Luke 12:32

For God did not give us a spirit of timidity, but a spirit of power, of love and of self-discipline.

II Timothy 1:7

There is no fear in love. But perfect love drives out fear, because fear has to do with punishment. The one who fears is not made perfect in love.

I John 4:18

Deal with Your Frustrations Properly

In your anger do not sin; when you are on your beds, search your hearts and be silent.

Psalm 4:4

Do not let the sun go down while you are still angry.

Ephesians 4:26b

Surely it was for my benefit that I suffered such anguish. In your love you kept me from the pit of destruction; you have put all my sins behind your back.

Isaiah 38:17

Get rid of all bitterness, rage and anger, brawling and slander, along with every form of malice.

Ephesians 4:31

See to it that no one misses the grace of God and that no bitter root grows up to cause trouble and defile many.

Hebrews 12:15

Don't Let Worry Take Over

I tell you, do not worry about your life, what you will eat or drink; or about your body, what you will wear. Is not life more important than food, and the body more important than clothes? Look at the birds of the air; they do not sow or reap or store away in barns, and yet your heavenly Father feeds them. Are you not much more valuable than they? Who of you by worrying can add a single hour to his life? And why do you worry about clothes? See how the lilies of the field grow. They do not labor or spin. Yet I tell you that not even Solomon in all his splendor was dressed like one of these. If that is how God clothes the grass of the field, which is here today and tomorrow is thrown into the fire, will he not much more clothe you, O you of little faith? So do not worry, saying, "What shall we eat?" or "What shall we drink?" or "What shall we wear?"

For the pagans run after all these things, and your heavenly Father knows that you need them. But seek first his kingdom and his righteousness, and all these things will be given to you as well. Therefore do not worry about tomorrow, for tomorrow will worry about itself. Each day has enough trouble of its own.

Matthew 6:25-34

Do not be anxious about anything, but in everything, by prayer and petition, with thanksgiving, present your requests to God. And the peace of God, which transcends all understanding, will guard your hearts and your minds in Christ Jesus. I am not saying this because I am in need, for I have learned to be content whatever the circumstances. I know what it is to be in need, and I know what it is to have plenty. I have learned the secret of being content in any and every situation, whether well fed or hungry, whether living in plenty or in want.

Philippians 4:6,7,11,12

BIBLE WISDOM FOR PARENTS

You Are Not a Failure!

I know that nothing good lives in me, that is, in my sinful nature. For I have the desire to do what is good, but I cannot carry it out. For what I do is not the good I want to do; no, the evil I do not want to do—this I keep on doing. Now if I do what I do not want to do, it is no longer I who do it, but it is sin living in me that does it.

Romans 7:18-20

The LORD is close to the brokenhearted and saves those who are crushed in spirit.

Psalm 34:18

I will exalt you, O LORD,
for you lifted me out of the depths
and did not let my enemies gloat over me.
O LORD my God,
I called to you for help and you healed me.
O LORD, you brought me up from the grave;
you spared me from going down into the pit.
Sing to the LORD, you saints of his;

praise his holy name.
For his anger lasts only a moment,
but his favor lasts a lifetime;
weeping may remain for a night,
but rejoicing comes in the morning.

Psalm 30:1-5

Cast your cares on the LORD and he will sustain you;
he will never let the righteous fall.

Psalm 55:22

He heals the brokenhearted and binds up their
wounds.

Psalm 147:3

Strengthen the feeble hands, steady the knees that
give way; say to those with fearful hearts, "Be strong,
do not fear; your God will come.

Psalm 35:3

When you pass through the waters, I will be with
you; and when you pass through the rivers, they will
not sweep over you. When you walk through the
fire, you will not be burned; the flames will not set
you ablaze.

Isaiah 43:2

•Accept Your Limitations

If anyone thinks he is something when he is nothing, he deceives himself.

-Galatians 6:3

Show me, O LORD, my life's end and the number of my days; let me know how fleeting is my life.

Psalm 39:4

As for men, God tests them
so that they may see that they are like the animals.
Man's fate is like that of the animals;
the same fate awaits them both:
As one dies, so dies the other.
All have the same breath;
man has no advantage over the animal.
Everything is meaningless.
All go to the same place;
all come from dust, and to dust all return.

Ecclesiastes 3:18-20

I have seen something else under the sun:
The race is not to the swift or the battle to the strong,
nor does food come to the wise
or wealth to the brilliant or favor to the learned;
but time and chance happen to them all.

Moreover, no man knows when his hour will come:
As fish are caught in a cruel net,
or birds are taken in a snare,
so men are trapped by evil times that fall unexpect-
edly upon them.

Ecclesiastes 9:11, 12

But we have this treasure in jars of clay to show that
this all-surpassing power is from God and not from
us. We are hard pressed on every side, but not
crushed; perplexed, but not in despair; persecuted,
but not abandoned; struck down, but not destroyed.
We always carry around in our body the death of
Jesus, so that the life of Jesus may also be revealed
in our body. For we who are alive are always being
given over to death for Jesus' sake, so that his life
may be revealed in our mortal body.

II Corinthians 4:7-11

Come to me, all you who are weary and burdened,
and I will give you rest. Take my yoke upon you and
learn from me, for I am gentle and humble in heart,
and you will find rest for your souls. For my yoke is
easy and my burden is light.

Matthew 11:28-30

Finally, be strong in the Lord and in his mighty power.

Ephesians 6:10

• Seek God's Peace

You will keep in perfect peace him whose mind is steadfast, because he trusts in you.

Isaiah 26:3

He will be like a tree planted by the water that sends out its roots by the stream. It does not fear when heat comes; its leaves are always green. It has no worries in a year of drought and never fails to bear fruit.

Jeremiah 17:8

Peace I leave with you; my peace I give you. I do not give to you as the world gives. Do not let your hearts be troubled and do not be afraid.

John 14:27

I have told you these things, so that in me you may have peace. In this world you will have trouble. But take heart! I have overcome the world.

John 16:33

111

For God is not a God of disorder but of peace.

I Corinthians 14:33

For he himself is our peace, who has made the two one and has destroyed the barrier, the dividing wall of hostility, by abolishing in his flesh the law with its commandments and regulations. His purpose was to create in himself one new man out of the two, thus making peace, and in this one body to reconcile both of them to God through the cross, by which he put to death their hostility. He came and preached peace to you who were far away and peace to those who were near.

Ephesians 2:14-17

Now may the Lord of peace himself give you peace at all times and in every way. The Lord be with all of you.

II Thessalonians 3:16

FOR PERSONAL PRAYER:

Lord, I get so close to being overwhelmed by the demands of job and family. Refresh me this day with Your peace and strength. Help me to know, in very practical ways, that You are upholding me as I seek to raise my children according to Your will. Amen.

CHAPTER 7

'Where will the money come from, Lord?'

I never seem to be able to get over the hump," said Chris, a single parent. "Just when I'm getting a little savings together, some crisis hits—the car breaks down, or something—and there goes the extra money.

"I don't have much trouble relating to my children, and they know I love them. But just keeping them clothed and fed is pushing me to the limits."

FOR MEMORY:

Listen, my dear brothers: Has not God chosen those who are poor in the eyes of the world to be rich in faith and to inherit the kingdom he promised those who love him?

James 2:5

FOR SILENT REFLECTION:

- *How important has the pursuit of money become in my life?*

- *What does it mean for me to rely on God to meet my family's needs?*

- *In what ways am I teaching my children the value of things other than money or possessions?*

- *How could I work on handling my worry with more faith in God's care and concern?*

When Your Family Expenses Weigh You Down . . .

The LORD hears the needy.

Psalm 69:33a

He will judge your people in righteousness,
your afflicted ones with justice.
The mountains will bring prosperity to the people,
the hills the fruit of righteousness.
He will defend the afflicted among the people
and save the children of the needy;
he will crush the oppressor.
For he will deliver the needy who cry out,
the afflicted who have no one to help.
He will take pity on the weak and the needy
and save the needy from death.

Psalm 72:2-4, 12, 13

For he stands at the right hand of the needy one, to
save his life from those who condemn him.

Psalm 109:31

I will bless her with abundant provisions; her poor
will I satisfy with food.

Psalm 132:15

Do not exploit the poor because they are poor
and do not crush the needy in court,
for the LORD will take up their case
and will plunder those who plunder them.

Proverbs 22:22, 23

The poor and needy search for water, but there is
none; their tongues are parched with thirst. But I the
LORD will answer them; I, the God of Israel, will not
forsake them.

Isaiah 41:17

Listen, my dear brothers: Has not God chosen those
who are poor in the eyes of the world to be rich in
faith and to inherit the kingdom he promised those
who love him?

James 2:5

• Trust in God's Provision
The eternal God is your refuge, and underneath are
the everlasting arms. He will drive out your enemy
before you, saying, 'Destroy him!'

Deuteronomy 33:27

He will guard the feet of his saints, but the wicked will be silenced in darkness. It is not by strength that one prevails.

I Samuel 2:9

Fear the LORD, you his saints,
for those who fear him lack nothing.
The lions may grow weak and hungry,
but those who seek the LORD lack no good thing.

Psalm 34:9, 10

The LORD will keep you from all harm—
he will watch over your life;
the LORD will watch over your coming
and going both now and forevermore.

Psalm 121:7, 8

I was young and now I am old, yet I have never seen the righteous forsaken or their children begging bread.

Psalm 37:25

"I tell you the truth," Jesus replied, "no one who has left home or brothers or sisters or mother or father or children or fields for me and the gospel will fail to receive a hundred times as much in this present age (homes, brothers, sisters, mothers, children and fields—and with them, persecutions) and in the age to come, eternal life.

Mark 10:29, 30

And God is able to make all grace abound to you, so that in all things at all times, having all that you need, you will abound in every good work.

II Corinthians 9:8

And my God will meet all your needs according to his glorious riches in Christ Jesus.

Philippians 4:19

Cast all your anxiety on him because he cares for you.

I Peter 5:7

• *Honor God with Your Money*

Honor the LORD with your wealth,
with the firstfruits of all your crops;
then your barns will be filled to overflowing,
and your vats will brim over with new wine.

-Proverbs 3:9, 10

Do not wear yourself out to get rich;
have the wisdom to show restraint.
Cast but a glance at riches, and they are gone,
for they will surely sprout wings
and fly off to the sky like an eagle.

Proverbs 23:4, 5

Jesus told his disciples: "There was a rich man whose manager was accused of wasting his possessions. So he called him in and asked him, 'What is this I hear about you? Give an account of your management, because you cannot be manager any longer.'

"The manager said to himself, 'What shall I do now? My master is taking away my job. I'm not strong enough to dig, and I'm ashamed to beg—I know what I'll do so that, when I lose my job here, people will welcome me into their houses.'

"So he called in each one of his master's debtors. He asked the first, 'How much do you owe my master?' 'Eight hundred gallons of olive oil,' he replied. The manager told him, 'Take your bill, sit down quickly, and make it four hundred.' Then he asked the second, 'And how much do you owe?' 'A thousand bushels of wheat,' he replied. He told him, 'Take your bill and make it eight hundred.' The master commended the dishonest manager because he had acted shrewdly.

"For the people of this world are more shrewd in dealing with their own kind than are the people of the light. I tell you, use worldly wealth to gain friends for yourselves, so that when it is gone, you will be welcomed into eternal dwellings.

"Whoever can be trusted with very little can also be trusted with much, and whoever is dishonest with very little will also be dishonest with much. So if you have not been trustworthy in handling worldly wealth, who will trust you with true riches? And if you have not been trustworthy with someone else's property, who will give you property of your own?

"No servant can serve two masters. Either he will hate the one and love the other, or he will be devoted to the one and despise the other. You cannot serve both God and Money."

Luke 16:1-13

So then, men ought to regard us as servants of Christ and as those entrusted with the secret things of God. Now it is required that those who have been given a trust must prove faithful.

I Corinthians 4:1, 2

• Don't Make Money Your Primary Concern

Do not store up for yourselves treasures on earth, where moth and rust destroy, and where thieves break in and steal. But store up for yourselves treasures in heaven, where moth and rust do not destroy, and where thieves do not break in and steal. For where your treasure is, there your heart will be also. The eye is the lamp of the body. If your eyes are good, your whole body will be full of light. But if your eyes are bad, your whole body will be full of darkness. If then the light within you is darkness, how great is that darkness! No one can serve two masters. Either he will hate the one and love the other, or he will be devoted to the one and despise the other. You cannot serve both God and Money.

Matthew 6:19-24

But godliness with contentment is great gain. For we brought nothing into the world, and we can take nothing out of it. But if we have food and clothing, we will be content with that. People who want to get rich fall into temptation and a trap and into many foolish and harmful desires that plunge men into ruin and destruction. For the love of money is a root of all kinds of evil. Some people, eager for money, have wandered from the faith and pierced themselves

with many griefs. But you, man of God, flee from all
this, and pursue righteousness, godliness, faith, love,
endurance and gentleness.

I Timothy 6:6-11

And he told them this parable: "The ground of a certain rich man produced a good crop. He thought to
himself, 'What shall I do? I have no place to store my
crops.' Then he said, 'This is what I'll do. I will tear
down my barns and build bigger ones, and there I
will store all my grain and my goods. And I'll say to
myself, "You have plenty of good things laid up for
many years. Take life easy; eat, drink and be merry.'
"But God said to him, 'You fool! This very night your
life will be demanded from you. Then who will get
what you have prepared for yourself?' This is how it
will be with anyone who stores up things for himself
but is not rich toward God."

Luke 12:16-21

• Don't Covet What Others Have

Watch out! Be on your guard against all kinds of
greed; a man's life does not consist in the abundance
of his possessions.

Luke 12:15a

You shall not covet your neighbor's house. You shall not covet your neighbor's wife, or his manservant or maidservant, his ox or donkey, or anything that belongs to your neighbor.

Exodus 20:17

Humility and the fear of the LORD bring wealth and honor and life.

Proverbs 22:4

For riches do not endure forever, and a crown is not secure for all generations.

Proverbs 27:24

The brother in humble circumstances ought to take pride in his high position. But the one who is rich should take pride in his low position, because he will pass away like a wild flower. For the sun rises with scorching heat and withers the plant; its blossom falls and its beauty is destroyed. In the same way, the rich man will fade away even while he goes about his business.

James 1:9-11

• Try to Help Others in Need, Too

If there is a poor man among your brothers in any of the towns of the land that the LORD your God is giving you, do not be hardhearted or tightfisted toward your poor brother. Rather be openhanded and freely lend him whatever he needs. Give generously to him and do so without a grudging heart; then because of this the LORD your God will bless you in all your work and in everything you put your hand to. There will always be poor people in the land. Therefore I command you to be openhanded toward your brothers and toward the poor and needy in your land.

Deuteronomy 15:7, 8, 10, 11

Blessed is he who has regard for the weak; the LORD delivers him in times of trouble.

Psalms 41:1

A generous man will himself be blessed, for he shares his food with the poor.

Proverbs 22:9

Give to the one who asks you, and do not turn away from the one who wants to borrow from you.

Matthew 5:42

So when you give to the needy, do not announce it with trumpets, as the hypocrites do in the synagogues and on the streets, to be honored by men. I tell you the truth, they have received their reward in full. But when you give to the needy, do not let your left hand know what your right hand is doing, so that your giving may be in secret. Then your Father, who sees what is done in secret, will reward you.

Matthew 6:2-4

But just as you excel in everything—in faith, in speech, in knowledge, in complete earnestness and in your love for us—see that you also excel in this grace of giving.

II Corinthians 8:7

Remember this: Whoever sows sparingly will also reap sparingly, and whoever sows generously will also reap generously. Each man should give what he has decided in his heart to give, not reluctantly or under compulsion, for God loves a cheerful giver. And God is able to make all grace abound to you, so that in all things at all times, having all that you need, you will abound in every good work. As it is written: "He has scattered abroad his gifts to the poor; his righteousness endures forever."

Now he who supplies seed to the sower and bread for food will also supply and increase your store of seed and will enlarge the harvest of your righteousness. You will be made rich in every way so that you can be generous on every occasion, and through us your generosity will result in thanksgiving to God. This service that you perform is not only supplying the needs of God's people but is also overflowing in many expressions of thanks to God.

II Corinthians 9:6-12

If anyone has material possessions and sees his brother in need but has no pity on him, how can the love of God be in him? Dear children, let us not love with words or tongue but with actions and in truth. This then is how we know that we belong to the truth, and how we set our hearts at rest in his presence.

I John 3:17-19

Jesus sat down opposite the place where the offerings were put and watched the crowd putting their money into the temple treasury. Many rich people threw in large amounts. But a poor widow came and put in two very small copper coins, worth only a fraction of a penny. Calling his disciples to him, Jesus said, "I tell you the truth, this poor widow has put more into the treasury than all the others. They all gave out of their wealth; but she, out of her poverty, put in everything—all she had to live on."

Mark 12:41-44

Do not be afraid, little flock, for your Father has been pleased to give you the kingdom. Sell your possessions and give to the poor. Provide purses for yourselves that will not wear out, a treasure in heaven that will not be exhausted, where no thief comes near and no moth destroys. For where your treasure is, there your heart will be also.

Luke 12:32-34

FOR PERSONAL PRAYER:

Lord, so often I worry about money. Yet, I know that no matter how much money I have, I still need to find my ultimate security in You alone. Give me perspective when the bills come in each month. And guide me into creative ways to balance my budget. Amen.

═══ CHAPTER 8 ═══

'Why do I feel so alone in my parenting struggles?'

B efore Dan and I got into a small group at church,
we didn't have anywhere to turn for parenting
advice," said Maria. "Both of our own parents
lived hundreds of miles away, and we had just relocated
to a brand-new neighborhood. We really felt lost."

"That's right," added Dan. "But then we joined a
group that focuses on the issues parents face in rais-
ing kids. It was like a breath of fresh air. We shared
everything, our frustrations and our successes. I'd say
we came away from each meeting with at least one
new idea to try out in our home. Not to mention the
fact that we built some lasting friendships with other
young parents."

FOR MEMORY:

I, the LORD, have called you in righteousness;
I will take hold of your hand.

Isaiah 42:6a

FOR SILENT REFLECTION:

- *How do I typically respond when I feel left alone or confused about what to do?*

- *Do I ever feel that I must "go it alone" as a parent?*

- *What expanded roles could my parents or other relatives play in helping raise my children?*

- *In what ways have I sought closer fellowship with God and His people lately?*

Feeling Lonely As a Parent?

I looked for sympathy, but there was none, for comforters, but I found none.

Psalm 69:20b

And now my life ebbs away;
days of suffering grip me.
Night pierces my bones;
my gnawing pains never rest.
In his great power God becomes like clothing to me;
he binds me like the neck of my garment.
He throws me into the mud,
and I am reduced to dust and ashes.
I cry out to you, O God, but you do not answer;
I stand up, but you merely look at me.

Job 30:16-20

I, the LORD, have called you in righteousness; I will take hold of your hand. I will keep you and will make you to be a covenant for the people and a light for the Gentiles.

Isaiah 42:6

For the LORD will not reject his people; he will never forsake his inheritance.

Psalm 94:14

133

"Though the mountains be shaken and the hills be removed, yet my unfailing love for you will not be shaken nor my covenant of peace be removed," says the LORD, who has compassion on you.

Isaiah 54:10

God has said, "Never will I leave you; never will I forsake you."

Hebrews 13:5b

• *Build a Support Network of Other Parents*

How good and pleasant it is
when brothers live together in unity!
It is like precious oil poured on the head,
running down on the beard,
running down on Aaron's beard,
down upon the collar of his robes.
It is as if the dew of Hermon were falling on Mount Zion.
For there the LORD bestows
his blessing, even life forevermore.

Psalm 133:1-3

When Job's three friends, Eliphaz the Temanite, Bildad the Shuhite and Zophar the Naamathite, heard about all the troubles that had come upon him, they set out from their homes and met together by agreement to go and sympathize with him and comfort him.

When they saw him from a distance, they could hardly recognize him; they began to weep aloud, and they tore their robes and sprinkled dust on their heads. Then they sat on the ground with him for seven days and seven nights. No one said a word to him, because they saw how great his suffering was.

Job 2:11-13

Be devoted to one another in brotherly love. Honor one another above yourselves.

Romans 12:10

Therefore encourage one another and build each other up, just as in fact you are doing. And we urge you, brothers, warn those who are idle, encourage the timid, help the weak, be patient with everyone.

I Thessalonians 5:11, 14

Therefore encourage each other with these words.

I Thessalonians 4:18

• Find Support in Your Church

Let us not give up meeting together, as some are in the habit of doing, but let us encourage one another—and all the more as you see the Day approaching.

Hebrews 10:25

The body is a unit, though it is made up of many parts; and though all its parts are many, they form one body. So it is with Christ. For we were all baptized by one Spirit into one body—whether Jews or Greeks, slave or free—and we were all given the one Spirit to drink.

Now the body is not made up of one part but of many. If the foot should say, "Because I am not a hand, I do not belong to the body," it would not for that reason cease to be part of the body. And if the ear should say, "Because I am not an eye, I do not belong to the body," it would not for that reason cease to be part of the body. If the whole body were an eye, where would the sense of hearing be? If the whole body were an ear, where would the sense of smell be?

But in fact God has arranged the parts in the body, every one of them, just as he wanted them to be. If they were all one part, where would the body be? As it is, there are many parts, but one body. The eye cannot say to the hand, "I don't need you!" And the head cannot say to the feet, "I don't need you!"

On the contrary, those parts of the body that seem to be weaker are indispensable, and the parts that we think are less honorable we treat with special honor. And the parts that are unpresentable are treated with special modesty, while our presentable parts need no special treatment. But God has combined the members of the body and has given greater honor to the parts that lacked it, so that there should be no division in the body, but that its parts should have equal concern for each other.

If one part suffers, every part suffers with it; if one part is honored, every part rejoices with it.

I Corinthians 12:12-26

They devoted themselves to the apostles' teaching and to the fellowship, to the breaking of bread and to prayer. Everyone was filled with awe, and many wonders and miraculous signs were done by the apostles. All the believers were together and had everything in common. Selling their possessions and goods, they gave to anyone as he had need. Every day they continued to meet together in the temple courts. They broke bread in their homes and ate together with glad and sincere hearts, praising God and enjoying the favor of all the people. And the Lord added to their number daily those who were being saved.

Acts 2:42-47

There is one body and one Spirit—just as you were called to one hope when you were called—one Lord, one faith, one baptism; one God and Father of all, who is over all and through all and in all.

Ephesians 4:4-6

If anyone says, "I love God," yet hates his brother, he is a liar. For anyone who does not love his brother, whom he has seen, cannot love God, whom he has not seen. And he has given us this command: Whoever loves God must also love his brother.

I John 4:20, 21

• *Support One Another with Your Gifts*
There are different kinds of gifts, but the same Spirit. There are different kinds of service, but the same Lord. There are different kinds of working, but the same God works all of them in all men. Now to each one the manifestation of the Spirit is given for the common good. To one there is given through the

Spirit the message of wisdom, to another the message of knowledge by means of the same Spirit, to another faith by the same Spirit, to another gifts of healing by that one Spirit, to another miraculous powers, to another prophecy, to another distinguishing between spirits, to another speaking in different kinds of tongues, and to still another the interpretation of tongues. All these are the work of one and the same Spirit, and he gives them to each one, just as he determines.

I Corinthians 12:4-11

But to each one of us grace has been given as Christ apportioned it. It was he who gave some to be apostles, some to be prophets, some to be evangelists, and some to be pastors and teachers, to prepare God's people for works of service, so that the body of Christ may be built up until we all reach unity in the faith and in the knowledge of the Son of God and become mature, attaining to the whole measure of the fullness of Christ. Then we will no longer be infants, tossed back and forth by the waves, and blown here and there by every wind of teaching and by the cunning and craftiness of men in their deceitful scheming. Instead, speaking the truth in love, we will in all things grow up into him who is the Head, that is, Christ. From him the whole body, joined and held together by every supporting ligament, grows and builds itself up in love, as each part does its work.

Ephesians 4:7, 11-16

Above all, love each other deeply, because love covers over a multitude of sins. Offer hospitality to one another without grumbling. Each one should use whatever gift he has received to serve others, faithfully administering God's grace in its various forms. If anyone speaks, he should do it as one speaking the very words of God. If anyone serves, he should do it with the strength God provides, so that in all things God may be praised through Jesus Christ. To him be the glory and the power for ever and ever. Amen.

I Peter 4:8-11

Learn to Fellowship with God in Prayer

The LORD is near to all who call on him, to all who call on him in truth. He fulfills the desires of those who fear him; he hears their cry and saves them.

Psalm 145:18, 19

Then you will call, and the LORD will answer; you will cry for help, and he will say: Here am I. If you do away with the yoke of oppression, with the pointing finger and malicious talk.

Isaiah 58:9

Let us draw near to God with a sincere heart in full assurance of faith, having our hearts sprinkled to cleanse us from a guilty conscience and having our bodies washed with pure water.

Hebrews 10:22

Ask and it will be given to you; seek and you will find; knock and the door will be opened to you. For everyone who asks receives; he who seeks finds; and to him who knocks, the door will be opened. Which of you, if his son asks for bread, will give him a stone?

Or if he asks for a fish, will give him a snake? If you, then, though you are evil, know how to give good gifts to your children, how much more will your Father in heaven give good gifts to those who ask him!

Matthew 7:7-11

If you remain in me and my words remain in you, ask whatever you wish, and it will be given you. This is to my Father's glory, that you bear much fruit, showing yourselves to be my disciples. As the Father has loved me, so have I loved you. Now remain in my love. If you obey my commands, you will remain in my love, just as I have obeyed my Father's commands and remain in his love. I have told you this so that my joy may be in you and that your joy may be complete. My command is this: Love each other as I have loved you. Greater love has no one than this, that he lay down his life for his friends. You are my friends if you do what I command. I no longer call you servants, because a servant does not know his master's business. Instead, I have called you friends, for everything that I learned from my Father I have made known to you. You did not choose me, but I chose you and appointed you to go and bear fruit— fruit that will last. Then the Father will give you whatever you ask in my name.

John 15:7-16

• God Hears Your Prayers

This is the confidence we have in approaching God: that if we ask anything according to his will, he hears us.

I John 5:14

Before they call I will answer; while they are still speaking I will hear.

Isaiah 65:24

Call to me and I will answer you and tell you great and unsearchable things you do not know.

Jeremiah 33:3

If any of you lacks wisdom, he should ask God, who gives generously to all without finding fault, and it will be given to him.

James 1:5

Then Hannah prayed and said: "My heart rejoices in the LORD; in the LORD my horn is lifted high. My mouth boasts over my enemies, for I delight in your deliverance. . . .And the LORD was gracious to Hannah; she conceived and gave birth to three sons and two daughters. Meanwhile, the boy Samuel grew up in the presence of the LORD.

I Samuel 2:1, 21

If my people, who are called by my name, will humble themselves and pray and seek my face and turn from their wicked ways, then will I hear from heaven and will forgive their sin and will heal their land.

II Chronicles 7:14

Yet if you devote your heart to him and stretch out your hands to him, if you put away the sin that is in your hand and allow no evil to dwell in your tent, then you will lift up your face without shame; you will stand firm and without fear. You will surely forget your trouble, recalling it only as waters gone by. Life will be brighter than noonday, and darkness will become like morning. You will be secure, because there is hope; you will look about you and take your rest in safety. You will lie down, with no one to make you afraid, and many will court your favor.

Job 11:13-19

Who among you fears the LORD and obeys the word of his servant? Let him who walks in the dark, who has no light, trust in the name of the LORD and rely on his God.

Isaiah 50:10

•*God's Spirit Dwells Within You*
I will pour out my Spirit on all people.
Your sons and daughters will prophesy,
your old men will dream dreams,
your young men will see visions.
Even on my servants, both men and women,
I will pour out my Spirit in those days.

144

I will show wonders in the heavens and on the earth,
blood and fire and billows of smoke.
The sun will be turned to darkness
and the moon to blood
before the coming of the great and dreadful day of
the LORD.
And everyone who calls on the name of the LORD
will be saved;
for on Mount Zion and in Jerusalem there will be
deliverance,
as the LORD has said, among the survivors whom
the LORD calls.

Joel 2:28b-32

If you then, though you are evil, know how to give
good gifts to your children, how much more will
your Father in heaven give the Holy Spirit to those
who ask him!"

Luke 11:13

On the last and greatest day of the Feast, Jesus stood
and said in a loud voice, "If anyone is thirsty, let him
come to me and drink. Whoever believes in me, as
the Scripture has said, streams of living water will
flow from within him." By this he meant the Spirit,
whom those who believed in him were later to

145

receive. Up to that time the Spirit had not been given, since Jesus had not yet been glorified.

John 7:37-39

All this I have spoken while still with you. But the Counselor, the Holy Spirit, whom the Father will send in my name, will teach you all things and will remind you of everything I have said to you. Peace I leave with you; my peace I give you. I do not give to you as the world gives. Do not let your hearts be troubled and do not be afraid.

John 14:25-27

Now I am going to him who sent me, yet none of you asks me, 'Where are you going?' Because I have said these things, you are filled with grief. But I tell you the truth: It is for your good that I am going away. Unless I go away, the Counselor will not come to you; but if I go, I will send him to you. When he comes, he will convict the world of guilt in regard to sin and righteousness and judgment: in regard to sin, because men do not believe in me; in regard to righteousness, because I am going to the Father, where you can see me no longer; and in regard to judgment, because the prince of this world now stands condemned. I have much more to say to you, more than you can now bear. But when he, the Spirit of truth, comes, he will guide you into all truth. He will not speak on his own; he will speak only what he hears, and he will tell you what is yet to come. He will bring glory to me by taking from what is mine and making it known to you. All that belongs to the Father is mine. That is why I said the Spirit will take from what is mine and make it known to you.

John 16:5-15

FOR PERSONAL PRAYER:

Even though I'm often surrounded by friends and family, I know that only I can be my child's parent. Sometimes this makes me feel lonely, Lord—especially when I don't know exactly what to do. Give me Your insight, and direct me to others who can lend support, too. Amen.

147

CHAPTER 9

'What do I do when parenting stress builds up?'

I suppose it's not the kids that cause the real stress," says Julian. "It's the kids on top of everything else. I have to work hard at being aware of just what's bothering me, moment by moment, checking up on where the anger or frustration is coming from.

"Sometimes I'm working too hard and need more sleep. Sometimes I need to take time out for some exercise. Whatever the cause, I know that when stress builds to certain levels I'm more likely to take it out on the kids, to see them as 'problems' rather than the gifts to me that they really are."

FOR MEMORY:

I will lie down and sleep in peace, for you alone, O LORD, make me dwell in safety.

Psalm 4:8

FOR SILENT REFLECTION:

- *What are the causes of most of the stress I feel during a typical day? Can I do anything to make for more peace in those situations?*

- *How much sleep do I get each night? Is it enough?*

- *Do I actively look to God to meet my needs and calm life's storms?*

- *To what extent do my kids feel responsible for my stress levels? How can I help assure them that this is my problem, not theirs?*

Look at the Sources of Your Stress

• *Work Overload*

That same day Pharaoh gave this order to the slave drivers and foremen in charge of the people: "You are no longer to supply the people with straw for making bricks; let them go and gather their own straw. But require them to make the same number of bricks as before; don't reduce the quota. They are lazy; that is why they are crying out, 'Let us go and sacrifice to our God.' Make the work harder for the men so that they keep working and pay no attention to lies."

Then the slave drivers and the foremen went out and said to the people, "This is what Pharaoh says: 'I will not give you any more straw. Go and get your own straw wherever you can find it, but your work will not be reduced at all.'" So the people scattered all over Egypt to gather stubble to use for straw. The slave drivers kept pressing them, saying, "Complete the work required of you for each day, just as when you had straw."

Exodus 5:6-13

A man can do nothing better than to eat and drink and find satisfaction in his work. This too, I see, is from the hand of God.

Ecclesiastes 2:24

That everyone may eat and drink, and find satisfaction in all his toil—this is the gift of God.

Ecclesiastes 3:13

Then I realized that it is good and proper for a man to eat and drink, and to find satisfaction in his toilsome labor under the sun during the few days of life God has given him—for this is his lot. Moreover, when God gives any man wealth and possessions, and enables him to enjoy them, to accept his lot and be happy in his work—this is a gift of God.

Ecclesiastes 5:18, 19

• Family Tensions

Do you think I came to bring peace on earth? No, I tell you, but division. From now on there will be five in one family divided against each other, three against two and two against three. They will be divided, father against son and son against father, mother against daughter and daughter against mother,

mother-in-law against daughter-in-law and daughter-in-law against mother-in-law."

Luke 12:51-53

For I have come to turn 'a man against his father, a daughter against her mother, a daughter-in-law against her mother-in-law—a man's enemies will be the members of his own household.'

Matthew 10:35, 36

Jesus knew their thoughts and said to them, "Every kingdom divided against itself will be ruined, and every city or household divided against itself will not stand.

Matthew 12:25

• *Church Disputes*

What causes fights and quarrels among you? Don't they come from your desires that battle within you?

James 4:1

If any of you has a dispute with another, dare he take it before the ungodly for judgment instead of before the saints? Do you not know that the saints will judge the world? And if you are to judge the

world, are you not competent to judge trivial cases?
Do you not know that we will judge angels? How
much more the things of this life! Therefore, if you
have disputes about such matters, appoint as judges
even men of little account in the church! I say this to
shame you. Is it possible that there is nobody among
you wise enough to judge a dispute between believers? But instead, one brother goes to law against
another—and this in front of unbelievers! The very
fact that you have lawsuits among you means you
have been completely defeated already. Why not
rather be wronged? Why not rather be cheated?

I Corinthians 6:1-7

If your brother sins against you, go and show him
his fault, just between the two of you. If he listens to
you, you have won your brother over. But if he will
not listen, take one or two others along, so that
'every matter may be established by the testimony of
two or three witnesses.' If he refuses to listen to
them, tell it to the church; and if he refuses to listen
even to the church, treat him as you would a pagan
or a tax collector.

Matthew 18:15-17

If anyone wants to be contentious about this, we have no other practice—nor do the churches of God. In the following directives I have no praise for you, for your meetings do more harm than good. In the first place, I hear that when you come together as a church, there are divisions among you, and to some extent I believe it. No doubt there have to be differences among you to show which of you have God's approval.

I Corinthians 11:16-19

I am confident in the Lord that you will take no other view. The one who is throwing you into confusion will pay the penalty, whoever he may be. Brothers, if I am still preaching circumcision, why am I still being persecuted? In that case the offense of the cross has been abolished. As for those agitators, I wish they would go the whole way and emasculate themselves! You, my brothers, were called to be free. But do not use your freedom to indulge the sinful nature; rather, serve one another in love.

Galatians 5:10-13

It is true that some preach Christ out of envy and rivalry, but others out of goodwill.

Philippians 1:15

But if you harbor bitter envy and selfish ambition in your hearts, do not boast about it or deny the truth. Such "wisdom" does not come down from heaven but is earthly, unspiritual, of the devil. For where you have envy and selfish ambition, there you find disorder and every evil practice.

James 3:14-16

• Neighbors at Odds
The entire law is summed up in a single command: "Love your neighbor as yourself."

Galatians 5:14

Settle matters quickly with your adversary who is taking you to court. Do it while you are still with him on the way, or he may hand you over to the judge, and the judge may hand you over to the officer, and you may be thrown into prison. I tell you the truth, you will not get out until you have paid the last penny.

Matthew 5:25, 26

You have heard that it was said, 'Eye for eye, and tooth for tooth.' But I tell you, Do not resist an evil person. If someone strikes you on the right cheek, turn to him the other also. And if someone wants to sue you and take your tunic, let him have your cloak as well. If someone forces you to go one mile, go with him two miles.

Matthew 5:38-41

• *Project Frustrations*

When the enemies of Judah and Benjamin heard that the exiles were building a temple for the LORD, the God of Israel, they came to Zerubbabel and to the heads of the families and said, "Let us help you build because, like you, we seek your God and have been sacrificing to him since the time of Esarhaddon king of Assyria, who brought us here." But Zerubbabel, Jeshua and the rest of the heads of the families of Israel answered, "You have no part with us in building a temple to our God. We alone will build it for the LORD, the God of Israel, as King Cyrus, the king of Persia, commanded us." Then the peoples around them set out to discourage the people of Judah and make them afraid to go on building. They hired counselors to work against them and frustrate their plans during the entire reign of Cyrus king of Persia and down to the reign of Darius king of Persia.

Ezra 4:1-5

When Sanballat heard that we were rebuilding the wall, he became angry and was greatly incensed. He ridiculed the Jews, and in the presence of his associates and the army of Samaria, he said, "What are those feeble Jews doing? Will they restore their wall? Will they offer sacrifices? Will they finish in a day? Can they bring the stones back to life from those heaps of rubble—burned as they are?" Tobiah the Ammonite, who was at his side, said, "What they are building—if even a fox climbed up on it, he would break down their wall of stones!" Hear us, O our God, for we are despised. Turn their insults back on their own heads. Give them over as plunder in a land of captivity. Do not cover up their guilt or blot out their sins from your sight, for they have thrown insults in the face of the builders. . . .

After I looked things over, I stood up and said to the nobles, the officials and the rest of the people, "Don't be afraid of them. Remember the Lord, who is great and awesome . . . .

Nehemiah 4:1-14a

Take Care of Yourself!

If you listen carefully to the voice of the LORD your God and do what is right in his eyes, if you pay attention to his commands and keep all his decrees, I will not bring on you any of the diseases I brought on the Egyptians, for I am the LORD, who heals you.

Exodus 15:26

"I will restore you to health and heal your wounds," declares the LORD, "because you are called an outcast, Zion for whom no one cares."

Jeremiah 30:17

And the prayer offered in faith will make the sick person well; the Lord will raise him up. If he has sinned, he will be forgiven.

James 5:15

-Proverbs 9:5

-Luke 12:23

• Through Guarding Your Schedule
What I mean, brothers, is that the time is short.

I Corinthians 7:29a

Be wise in the way you act toward outsiders; make the most of every opportunity.

Colossians 4:5

159

Six days do your work, but on the seventh day do not work, so that your ox and your donkey may rest and the slave born in your household, and the alien as well, may be refreshed.

Exodus 23:12

But when God, who set me apart from birth and called me by his grace, was pleased to reveal his Son in me so that I might preach him among the Gentiles, I did not consult any man, nor did I go up to Jerusalem to see those who were apostles before I was, but I went immediately into Arabia and later returned to Damascus. Then after three years, I went up to Jerusalem. . . .

Galatians 1:15-18a

• *Through Getting Enough Rest*

I lie down and sleep; I wake again, because the LORD sustains me.

Psalm 3:5

I will lie down and sleep in peace, for you alone, O LORD, make me dwell in safety.

Psalm 4:8

160

Then [Jesus] got into the boat and his disciples followed him. Without warning, a furious storm came up on the lake, so that the waves swept over the boat. But Jesus was sleeping.

Matthew 8:23, 24

The apostles gathered around Jesus and reported to him all they had done and taught. Then, because so many people were coming and going that they did not even have a chance to eat, he said to them, "Come with me by yourselves to a quiet place and get some rest." So they went away by themselves in a boat to a solitary place.

Mark 6:30-32

• Through Asking God for Help

If you believe, you will receive whatever you ask for in prayer.

Matthew 21:22

Until now you have not asked for anything in my name. Ask and you will receive, and your joy will be complete.

John 16:24

161

Ask of me, and I will make the nations your inheritance, the ends of the earth your possession.

Psalm 2:8

This is what the LORD says: "Stand at the crossroads and look; ask for the ancient paths, ask where the good way is, and walk in it, and you will find rest for your souls. But you said, "We will not walk in it."

Jeremiah 6:16

Ask the LORD for rain in the springtime; it is the LORD who makes the storm clouds. He gives showers of rain to men, and plants of the field to everyone.

Zechariah 10:1

Again, I tell you that if two of you on earth agree about anything you ask for, it will be done for you by my Father in heaven.

Matthew 18:19

This is the confidence we have in approaching God: that if we ask anything according to his will, he hears us. And if we know that he hears us— whatever we ask—we know that we have what we asked of him.

I John 5:14, 15

Now to him who is able to do immeasurably more than all we ask or imagine, according to his power that is at work within us.

Ephesians 3:20

FOR PERSONAL PRAYER:

Jesus, even You experienced stress in Your daily life. But You always responded appropriately. That's what I want, too, especially when my kids come to me for nurture and I feel as though I have nothing to give. Fill my emotional and spiritual tanks, Lord, so I can in turn fill up my children with my love and Yours. Amen.

BIBLE WISDOM FOR MOTHERS

'Where can I turn for the courage and energy I need to be a good mom?'

'What if I've already made many mistakes parenting my kids?'

How can I raise my child's self-esteem?'

Bible Wisdom For Mothers helps to answer these and other questions often asked by caring, concerned moms by looking directly at the timeless wisdom of the Bible.

BIBLE WISDOM FOR FATHERS

'What if I never had a good, loving
father of my own for a role model?'

'How can I build my home on a solid
foundation of spiritual truth?'

'How can I handle my frustrations with
this incredible parenting challenge?'

Help in finding Biblical answers to these
and other questions commonly voiced by
dads everywhere can be found in *Bible Wisdom For Fathers*.

BIBLE WISDOM FOR SINGLE PARENTS

'How can I cope with this feeling of being so forsaken?'

'How can I keep my focus on God's goodness rather than on my problems?'

'How can I handle the stress of this balancing act?'

Discover what the Bible has to say in response to these and other important questions in *Bible Wisdom for Single Parents*.